Mavis Clan Barnett

April 1940

THE HEART OF ENGLAND

THE BRITISH HERITAGE SERIES

Uniform with this Volume. 7s. 6d. net each

THE SPIRIT OF LONDON
By PAUL COHEN-PORTHEIM

THE COUNTRYMAN'S ENGLAND
By DOROTHY HARTLEY

ENGLISH VILLAGES AND HAMLETS
By HUMPHREY PAKINGTON

THE OLD INNS OF ENGLAND
By A. E. RICHARDSON

THE CATHEDRALS OF ENGLAND
By HARRY BATSFORD and CHARLES FRY

THE PARISH CHURCHES OF ENGLAND
By J. CHARLES COX and C. BRADLEY FORD

THE FACE OF SCOTLAND
By HARRY BATSFORD and CHARLES FRY

THE HEART OF SCOTLAND
By GEORGE BLAKE

Published by
B. T. BATSFORD LTD.
15 North Audley Street, London, W.1.

1 LANCASHIRE COTTON MILLS

*From a Painting by
Sir Charles Holmes*

THE HEART OF
ENGLAND

By

IVOR BROWN

With a Foreword by
J. B. PRIESTLEY

LONDON
B. T. BATSFORD LTD.
15 NORTH AUDLEY STREET, W.1

attacking suburban and lower middle-class life, he goes too far in his reaction and is a little too optimistic. I for one feel less easy in mind about this new standardised Suburbia than he does. There is something tepid and passive about its life that worries me. I do not see men and women of character emerging in any great numbers from this Americanised urban life. And being more English than he is, I can tell him that I think he flatters us a little when he dwells upon our political good-humour and tolerance, contrasting them with the dark passions elsewhere. It is true that the English are kindly folk. But a good deal of what is praised as tolerance is merely indifference, based on a dwindling interest in politics and also on a false feeling of security. It is not so much that these people are monuments of patience and kindliness as that they do not really care about what is happening in public affairs. The same people make plenty of angry noises at football matches. And they can easily be stampeded—as more than one General Election has shown us—by artful catchpenny cries and nonsensical headlines in the popular Press.

These are, however, comparatively small differences of opinion. For once that I disagreed, I found myself agreeing twenty or thirty times, delightedly agreeing too. Here, within as small a compass as the subject could possibly allow, you have a lively panorama of contemporary England and English life, with a sensible and witty guide at your elbow. (This last phrase is tactless perhaps, for most of us detest having guides, no matter how sensible and witty, at our elbows. You have this guide, however, under control.) It is a book I would gladly hand over to any inquiring foreigner, though it is not so much the foreigner who needs it as those myriads of our own folk who should become better acquainted with their own country and the life that is lived in it. And the photographs, plentiful and well done, are worthy of the text. What Mr. Brown does not tell you, they will tell you. Between the two, you ought to have a grand time.

J. B. PRIESTLEY

An Oxford Haven

'TO many people of many lands it must have seemed something of a paradox that the new Bodleian buildings at Oxford should threaten the site and fabric of Blackwell's. They may have resigned themselves to upheaval and change at that corner of the Broad, but not, surely, to so dastardly a revolution as the shifting of their favourite bookshop or the modernising of its facial make-up. Their minds may rest in peace. The familiar Georgian front of Numbers 50 and 51 is to remain undisturbed. There has been some pulling down and reconstruction behind it and on its flank, and Ultima Thule no longer seems to be what it was: but Mr Basil Blackwell claims that here new conveniences outweigh a minor sacrifice of sentiment. In the nature of the site there cannot be so rude an expansion of space that customers will suffer from agoraphobia. The old soft hush will reign. The worst that will happen is that a visitor looking for books in a certain category may find them so easily as to lose the delights of counter-attractions and unwarranted expenditure as he pursues his search. Even for this Mr Basil Blackwell offers compensation in the maintenance of tradition. The country parson still can call at the shop in the morning, pick up a book, read through it then and there where he stands immobile, lay it down exactly where he found it, and depart for his tea or supper with assurance that he has hurt no one. Or presumably, if it is a little book, the undergraduate still may buy it, read it as he walks down the Broad, and sell it without loss, or perhaps with profit, over the way. The only risk he runs is that before he is out of Blackwell's he may be stopped and mistaken for one of the shop's staff. But that is a compliment few can afford to disdain.'—*Birmingham Post.*

BLACKWELL'S
48 - 51 Broad Street, Oxford

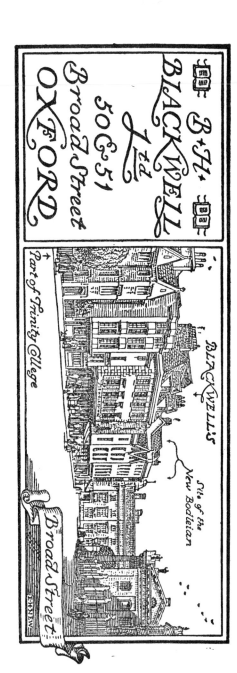

B·H·
BLACKWELL
Ltd
50 & 51
Broad Street
OXFORD

BLACKWELL'S

Site of the
New Bodleian

Part of Trinity College

Broad Street

ACKNOWLEDGMENT

The publishers must acknowledge their obligation to the photographers whose work is reproduced in these pages, namely, the late W. G. Davie, for fig. 67; Messrs. Aerofilms, Ltd., for figs. 4, 51; *Architecture Illustrated* for figs. 65, 68, 124; Mr. Graystone Bird, for fig. 22; Central Press Photos, for figs. 9, 19, 24, 28, 39, 77, 82, 91, 114, 117, 118, 119, 120; Mr. J. Dixon-Scott, for figs. 2, 14, 15, 26, 29, 36, 41, 43, 46, 52, 59, 60, 66, 79, 88; Mr. Herbert Felton, F.R.P.S., for figs. 13, 30, 31, 32, 42, 63, 64, 72, 95, 128, 129; Fox Photos, Ltd., for figs, 5, 6, 12, 20, 27, 40, 48, 49, 62, 69, 71, 73, 74, 78, 81, 83, 84, 85, 86, 90, 92, 97, 102, 103, 104, 105, 107, 108, 109, 110, 113, 116, 122, 125, 127; Messrs. Imperial Chemical Industries, Ltd., for fig. 53; Keystone View Co., for figs. 8, 11, 34, 35, 47, 50, 70, 76, 96, 111, 112, 115, 121; Mr. Hugh Quigley, for figs. 54, 56, 57; Sport & General Press Agency, for figs. 10, 25, 75, 87, 89, 98, 99, 100, 123; Mr. Will F. Taylor, for figs, 7, 18, 33, 37, 38, 44, 45, 58, 61, 80, 126; Topical Press Agency, for figs. 3, 16, 17, 23, 55, 93, 94, 101. Thanks are also due to Sir Charles Holmes for permission to reproduce the fine painting that appears as the frontispiece to this volume.

CONTENTS

2 LONDON RIVER

3   WEMBLEY CUP FINAL

THE HEART OF ENGLAND

CHAPTER I

INTRODUCTORY

IN any short book on a large subject the sins of omission are inevitably serious. In this case the task of selecting and omitting has been eased for me by the existence of volumes in the same series which cover certain areas of ground more fully and far better than I could hope to do. Readers will have very little from me about cathedral, church, and village architecture, about the beauty and history of the famous English inns and taverns, and about the capital itself. For these the publishers have wisely provided already. This book is a more random, vagabond affair, about life as it is lived in England, the social heritage and its new executors.

I have concerned myself a good deal with the leisure of the English, rather more, indeed, than with their labour. To generalise about nations or summarise epochs is always dangerous, but this, I think, may be said about contemporary England. The new age of the machine has assimilated our work and varied our recreation. While there are more and more people doing the same kind of job in the same kind of way, there are more and more who are existing more amply and freely when the job is done. Working hours have decreased; it is almost certain that working hours will decrease still further. We are confronted with a simultaneous growth of leisure and locomotion. The significant feature of English life to-day is its mobility. It is true that we rush ourselves to death upon the roads whose control has become a major concern of Government. But we do also carry ourselves on these same roads to better housing, better health, new and diverse pleasure, and wider knowledge and enjoyment of our country.

There has been much for the pessimist to set upon his side of the account. Town and regional planning have been loudly discussed, but, during the discussion, many a newly 'developed' area has been turned into confusion's masterpiece; mean 'ribbon' building and an anarchy of perky villadom have too often arrived before control could be arranged and enforced. The vigilant Societies, seeking to preserve the tranquil, the historical, and the beautiful, have been outrun by the speculator in sites and houses. But, however gloomily you may stress the 'uglification' of England, it seems to me indisputable that a great many English people are leading a better life than they would have done thirty years ago. We can admit the bitter regional depressions, the scandal of still-existing slums, and the continuing menace and oppression of life without work, of life, even, without much hope of work. But for nine-tenths of the population there is an ampler way of living. It is nothing to boast about. Standards of well-being bear as yet no proportion to the plenty which a machine-age can offer. But if we read the years not in the light of centuries only but of decades, we can find at least some opportunity for confidence. The expectation of life continually increases and so, at least in some respects, does the expectation of a good life. This is not an excuse for social complacence; it is only an attempt to interpret with fairness

4 THE GREEN CHEQUERBOARD

5 TRANSPORT AND POWER AT BATTERSEA

the records of sociological fact, which are not altogether gloomy.

Modern invention has been a great leveller. A machine may operate far more quickly than a political or economic measure to abolish privilege and wipe out the distinctions of class and finance. It is surely good that poor people can get far more recreation than they used to do and better value, not perhaps in actual goods, but in the conditions of using those goods. The 'slavey' class has almost vanished and been replaced by a smart and self-respecting young woman who goes to the same cinemas and takes her cup of tea amid the same marble as any other member of the community. Somebody should write a treatise on the Equalitarian Results of Artificial Silk. The factory-girl is no longer stamped as such. She is a woman-worker, like the girl who goes to an office. And when she is not working she has the means to enjoy herself. Superior people will observe that 'having a good time' may only involve some silly and trivial vanities and excitements. But the present argument is not concerned with the ethical and aesthetic values of superior people; it is concerned with the elementary facts of common wants in life and the achievement of those ends.

The Cinema has been another levelling force. In the old Victorian theatres the cheap seats were bare boards or little better; they were approached by stone passages or stone stairs which created the atmosphere of a work-house or a prison. The poor playgoer was segregated and made to feel poor; he had no access to the foyers. The audience was split up by class standards. When the Cinema began to capture the nation's pocket-money, it offered equalitarian pleasures. The poorest could have a comfortable seat and approach it over carpets without pauper-status. They were not labelled as a sixpenny rabble and driven down stone passages; they shared the glories of the glittering vestibule and were part-proprietors of the gold-fish in the one fountain, of the ice cream at the other. The old eating-houses of the poor proclaimed the poverty of their patrons; the new have more sumptuous decoration and more musical equipment than the restaurants of the rich. The domestic servant on her day out is not hustled away or driven to the mean streets because she only wants to spend sixpence on her tea. Nobody will claim that the nationalisation of marble halls and padded 'fauteuils' is vitally important: but it is significant. And broadcasting, with its level charge and same service for all, has been another great equalising force as well as an immense blessing to lonely people and those who cannot get about.

Cheap transport, again, has been a great liberator. Votes are one implement of enfranchisement; the motor-bicycle is another and the freedom which it confers may be more rapidly realised. Middle-class people, rather apt to regard the beauty and solitude of the countryside as their personal property, resent the crowds at 'beauty-spots' and the motor-coach upon the moors. I have frequently cursed the motor-cyclist who drives over country tracks and pelts across heaths and commons, leaving noise and smell in the midst of peace and solitude. But I realise that this young man and the girl upon the pillion are free in a way that their parents were not, free to be 'over the hills and far away' within an hour of leaving work in the town. Against the admitted evils of our time, the reckless urban expansion and the abuse of the countryside by its new invaders, we must set the advantages of an upward levelling in social standards and of the health and happiness which universal locomotion can offer. We hear much about the destruction of old beauty; let us remember that this is the first epoch in which preserving beauty was ever a matter of public policy. Our vandalism is at least challenged, if it is not always checked. Previous centuries had small conception of a heritage; they hacked and hewed as they pleased, shattering an Avebury, once the greatest megalithic temple in Europe, that some peasants might have free building stone, or permitting Shakespeare's New Place to vanish at a parson's whim.

So I make no apology for a certain note of optimism in this book. There are numbers of people who can tell us, often justly, what is wrong; amid their expostulation we may be deaf to certain elements of better news. That the death-rate of England has been very nearly halved in the last forty years, falling from 20·5 per 1,000 of population to 11·4, seems to me no inconsiderable fact. We live longer and in many ways more decently. There was a great deal of merriment in early Victorian England, at least according to Dickens. But it was largely based on heavy feeding and drinking. The poor man's oysters might mitigate his poverty, but what a universe of squalor and cruelty Dickens reveals! The torture and oppression of children, the savagery of punishments, the filth of the insanitary unlit streets create in me, at any rate, no nostalgic impulse. The heart of England was hard to touch in those days; it was more a gigantic callosity than an organ of the sentiments. We have far more scruple nowadays; a backward glance is flattering to the present survey; and so, not sadly, let us move forward to the street and the field.

CHAPTER II

SEAPORT AND SEASIDE

An island-nation wears its heart upon its sleeve. Geographically, the heart of England may be in the Midlands, industrially in the North, financially in London. But our history, like our commerce, has come and gone by the sea; through harbours of nature the Mediterranean men came with their long-boats to mine their flints and metals and leave the megalithic spoor of the first English civilisation; then the Celtic wave broke westward and the following Roman first stormed the Kentish shores, then held the Saxon. Through harbours builded into ports the subsequent cultures came seeping in and the English adventurers sailed out, later than the Spaniard, but never too late to land upon the Fortunate Isles of early dreamers and make these Hesperides a commercial proposition, a plunderer's paradise. Ships flowed out and wealth flowed back. From Europe came the priest, the craftsman, and the scholar as well as the warlord and his train. If the heart be the life-giver, we must begin at the seaside.

Rightly the capital of England is its greatest port; less rightly it is three-parts unconscious of the fact. The London worker, even if he travels daily from an eastern or south-eastern suburb, tumbles into the centre of things without much sense of maritime relations; considering its enormity and its vital importance London Harbour is a strangely secret place. The Port of London Authority rules the Thames from Teddington to the

6 TRADESMEN'S ENTRANCE: Ships unloading in the Upper Pool,
London

7 A STRANDED PORT : Rye Harbour

Nore, but the Thames to the average Londoner is not sea but river and, on the whole, a nuisance. It gets in his way; it might still be a highway, as it was of old, but now it is more of an obstruction; sometimes it floods, endangers, even drowns him. Unless he slides under it by a tube-tunnel, it is a thing to be crossed by a bridge, which means a tight neck for traffic and so delay.

In New York the mightiest liner may berth in the midst of the city; the syren adds to the mad music of the town. But London's Port is elusive; you may stand on London Bridge and see a Soviet vessel lading hard by; you may reflect that there are twenty miles of this on either bank, stretching away east to Gravesend (2). But people do not stand, as a rule, upon London Bridge; they bustle across to work or leisure and the twenty miles to Gravesend are rarely a matter for reflection. Besides, unless you really have an eye for ships and can pass for a dock-side specialist, it is apt to be disappointing. Docks often are.

The Londoner, if he is not by nature or employment a water-side man, must make a purposed and possibly exhausting journey to London Harbour if he is to see it at all with any thoroughness of comprehension. And how often does anybody set out to see his own town? Besides, if he does make the expedition, it is not easy for the unskilled wayfarer; he finds himself wandering up dingy lanes that are indistinguishable from inland slums, meets forbidding gates, is turned back, and tries again, until the rain comes on and he goes home. He ought, of course, to make inquiries first, to read his Tomlinson, to persevere; but he probably does not. In the summer he may take passage on a public vessel to Greenwich, with a view of balconied inns, such as the Prospect of Whitby, perched like happy nests of leisure, and past glum-looking steps that have been the gateways of historic adventure; it is a good outing for a sunlit afternoon; but noble Greenwich, after all, is only the beginning of the business. London, like England, wears its heart upon the sleeve; it is the sleeve of a very long arm and that sleeve, often disconcertingly shabby, is apt to be turned up. This heart is not so easy to discover. Still, he who has read his Tomlinson will be fired in the mind, and try again. I wish him better luck and a real victory over the London littoral of slums and tramlines (107).

The life of London Harbour has endured and increased; though it cannot take the largest vessels, its site is invincible. But other English harbours have had their ups and downs and ever will; the English coast has played its tricks; there was a time when the ships sailed up to Lewes; Rye stands, a sweet Acropolis, dear to the tourist and the golfer, but now bereft of ships (7); as the Channel fell back new towns, Seafords and Seatons, arose, and the old harbours found themselves stark and starving, inland villages on banks of inconsiderable rivers. The East coast is studded with derelict or diminished havens which now must cater rather for the amateur with his yacht than for the merchantman with his wares. Fortunately those which have ceased to receive cargo can often find holiday lodgers instead. Small fishing also yields to large, sail to steam, with curious and tragic depopulation as the result. The sea is a capricious foster-mother. You can always do something with most sorts of land. But, if the water departs or the trading shifts, there is only sand to be ploughed. Policy, too, may play

8 SOUTHAMPTON DOCKS

9 LIVERPOOL WATER FRONT

the deuce with a port. What will become of Chatham and
Portsmouth and Devonport if disarmament becomes a
drastic reality? But invention may add to the credit
balances. The 'motor-coaster,' carrying a large bulk on
a shallow draught, has recently helped the smaller and
older harbours. In 1923 only 101 ships arrived in the
ancient port of Norwich: in 1934 there were 628.

If you travel to New York on the pleasant, solid,
authentic ship, *Aquitania*, you will notice that the boats
on the boat-deck carry the Liverpool address. But you
did not start from Liverpool and you will not go back
there. The big ships have moved to Southampton, because for the Americans who want to go to Paris
Cherbourg is a handy port of call on the Southampton
route. Liverpool received its first charter from King John
and soared into power and prosperity when trade with
the Indies became one of England's great activities;
it is a tough-hearted place with an ever-growing population (9) and still has plenty to do; but it could do with
more and that loss of the luxury Atlantic business was
a heavy blow. Southampton is now, in terms of entering
and departing tonnage, the third English port. There
had to be a big migration of shipping folk, stewards and
sailors and marine workers of all kinds, to find new homes
in the rising, go-ahead Southampton. Yet the old loyal-
ties persist. When I was on the *Aquitania* I observed that
one of the most popular pieces of news (with the excellent people who did the work) was the Saturday wireless
which carried football results. What had Liverpool
done? A fig for Southampton! A man might have his
base there, but his heart would be elsewhere. Still that
will alter in time and Southampton certainly gives one

a gayer impression than Liverpool. It is a confident, head-in-the-air place now. And well it may be, spreading itself with great new docks, and eating its way inland to house the new myriads (8). The figures of population are informative. Between 1901 and 1911 the population of Southampton did not grow much beyond the normal standard of national increase; 104,911 became 119,012. Then came the war and the acquisition of the big liners. In 1921 the inhabitants had risen to 162,220, in 1931 to 176,025. By the time of the 1941 census Southampton's population will probably be approaching 200,000. Such are the ups and downs of harbour life.

Again, the vicissitudes of seaport life may depend upon the accident of a fish-tribe's movements or on the vagaries of the human appetite which desires or ceases to desire that form of food. East Anglian chronicles are written, so to speak, in herring-bone. Herrings were once currency on those shores; rents were paid in them and international affrays followed the Dutchmen's pursuit of the shoals into English waters. 'The fishery,' wrote Nashe of herrings in 1567, 'is a great nursery for seamen and brings more ships to Yarmouth than assembled at Troy to fetch back Paris.' That town had forty brewers in employ for thirsty fishers. But now the herring-trade, though great, does not suffice its workers. Appeals are made to Parliament and public for remedy; the first must act, the second must eat, that Yarmouth and many similar harbours, closely dependent on the herring, may be saved. Ups and downs.

The Port of London thrives on its generality of trade. A slump may scratch it severely, but the wound will not be deep enough to kill. It is a harder life for the ports

10, 11 THE HERRING FLEET, in Action and Repose

12 NOCTURNE AT HARWICH

13 LOBSTER-POTS AND HOLIDAY-MAKERS AT BERE, SOUTH DEVON

more closely dependent on specific freights; after the
war the coal-trade of Northumbria lost millions of tons
which had previously and regularly gone out to Germany,
Russia and France. But what the north-eastern harbours
lost in this way was to some extent recovered by developing, to the serious disadvantage of the railways, the coastal
trade with the southern harbours of our own country.
The old phrase sea-coal became apposite once more.
The export of coal from Blyth, for example, was over
five million tons in 1933 and over six million in 1934.
The coastwise trade took nearly four millions, three-
quarters of a million more than in the previous year.
About eighty per cent of this went to the Thames and
the Medway; much of the rest to the east of Scotland.
Some of the Thames coal is transhipped and taken right
up the river to Kingston. Coal is still the black heart of
England's industrial power, and here, too, we see the
heart worn upon the maritime sleeve.

Still, as single-minded men risk greater disillusion,
should their one faith or interest fail them, so the special-
ised harbour goes in danger of unmerited distress should
its staple suffer the buffets of economic fortune. Suppose
the Channel Tunnel had become a reality and trains
ran through it to the Continent. What would have been
the repercussions on Folkestone and Dover? It is note-
worthy (and surprising) that the tonnage entering and
leaving Dover is greater than that entering and leaving
Bristol, an historic harbour and natural gateway for the
Western trade. Sociological prophets may indulge their
fancy by speculating on the possible influence of aviation
on English harbours in fifty years' time. It can hardly
affect heavy cargoes; but already its intervention as a

carrier of mails and passengers must be vexatious to the shipping companies.

But Folkestone and Dover are not harbours only; they are seaside towns, possessing the peculiar quality and attractions of that kind. This brings us to quite another aspect of the maritime sleeve. The English way of living has found typical expression in its development of the '-on-Seas,' places where ships go by rather than places where ships come in. The seaside town, regarded as a dwelling-place and not as a harbour or a fort, was largely an eighteenth-century invention, and in the nineteenth and twentieth centuries it has proved increasingly popular. The first idea was to go to the sea for health, the second to go for fun; now many people, with no special ties, go there for a normal residence; the cost of living and especially of playing is so much cheaper than in London and its suburbs, and the climate is more sunny as a rule. The huge retired class, filtering back from all manner of work all over the Empire, many of its members pensioned while still in middle age and with good expectations of a long and easy but not an affluent life, have colonised the south coast thickly. To describe the English shore, from Dover to Penzance, as a suburb of India would be a jest containing some pith of actuality.

The English seaside town is a fascinating place for all possessed of an historical sense and social curiosity. It is like a canvas that has been painted over by many hands. It may, as in the case of Scarborough, begin with a Roman pavement, then turn to a medieval missal, then be formalised by the Foppingtons and the graceful hedonists of the eighteenth century, then suffer clumsy expansion by Victorian builders of the villa and the lodging-house, and finally be restored to some dignity by the more workmanlike contribution of the architects of to-day. It has been a harbour and become 'a resort,' Marine Parade replacing shabby waterfront, the Pleasure Pier the humble jetty. It may have been created from Georgian elegance, like Brighton (14), or it may, like Blackpool, be a village of the barren dunes transformed by the Kubla Khans of Victorian prosperity who did 'a stately Pleasure Dome decree' for the light relief and entertainment of their workers (16).

The typical seaside town of England usually begins with its Esplanade. Here are relics of a terrace in the classical style, old houses of the first colonists, retired merchants who had done well in the Indies trade. Many of these establishments, of sweet proportions and with charming fanlights on their doorways, are now converted into 'Private Hotels,' offering respectable shelter and very plain cooking at fifty shillings a week, or three guineas, if your bedroom has a sea view. They are flanked by the better lodging-houses, mid-Victorian stucco with coloured glass doorways and 'Bella Vista' titles. Behind are the shops, those happy seaside shops which, in summer-time, seem to burst in an ecstasy of holiday suggestion, with buckets and spades and all the gear of the beach projecting, like clustered bananas, into the narrow High Street. Behind the High Street are the cheaper lodging-houses, gaunt Victorian affairs with scabrous plaster on their brick. And then, further back, one finds the comfortable, well-gardened houses of 'the residents' (late of Calcutta, perhaps) who loathe the August crowds, keep themselves rigidly to themselves,

and jealously guard the golf and tennis clubs from the
contamination of pushing shop-keepers. Backward again,
as the little town slopes inward and upward, are the
new, small bungalows; behind them there may be an
occasional specimen of the modern 'functionalist' house,
of blanched aspect, a square, squat, utilitarian cover for
the rooms that are sparely furnished with the steely stuff
of the nineteen-thirties. The English seaside town can
be read at a glance. It is history in strips.

And happy history on the whole. The more respectable residents may seem sombre folk, with insufficient
occupation to keep them from tattle and scandal and
the pettiest recreation of intrigue. But what holiday-
making there has been! The English are a great people
for holidays. The summer seaside visit is a national
institution. The word 'tripper' is now reserved for the
casual invader with an excursion ticket and little else in
his purse, but in fact the English of all classes have been
'tripping' consistently since Sheridan's gentry 'tripped'
to Scarborough and Matt Bramble, experimenting with a
sea-bath, was all too forcibly rescued by Humphrey
Clinker. The *Margate Hoy*, Lamb's beloved vessel, had
become enormously popular by the beginning of the
nineteenth century; the 'rough accommodations' of the
Hoy were later replaced by the 'fresh-water niceness of
the modern steam-packet,' which carried prosperous City
folk to the Kentish resorts. 'Boz' has described this
human cargo richly, the stock-brokers, the novel-reading
spinster, the general atmosphere of sandwiches, brandy-
and-water, and genteel conversation on the Power of
Steam. In another of Dickens's early stories, *The Tuggses
at Ramsgate*, there is suggestion of the growing snobbery

14 BRIGHTON : Pier and Parade

15 SCARBOROUGH FROM THE OLD TOWN: Harbour and Holiday Resort

which made a sharp distinction between travelling and tripping, a distinction still actively maintained.

' "Gravesend?" mildly suggested Mr. Joseph Tuggs. The idea was unanimously scouted. Gravesend was *low*.

' "Margate?" insinuated Mrs. Tuggs. Worse and worse—nobody there but tradespeople.

' "Brighton?" Mr. Cymon Tuggs opposed an insurmountable objection. All the coaches had been upset, in turn, within the last three weeks; each coach had averaged two passengers killed and six wounded; and in every case, the newspapers had distinctly understood that "no blame whatever was attributable to the coachman."

' "Ramsgate?" ejaculated Mr. Cymon, thoughtfully. To be sure; how stupid they must have been not to have thought of that before! Ramsgate was just the place of all others.'

The reference to the Terrors of the Road, by the way, and to the exoneration of drivers is especially interesting in view of the present slaughter on the highway. There seems to have been abundant hazard even with the power of four real horses and long before the menace of 30 h.p. and 60 m.p.h.

At Ramsgate, finally achieved, life consisted of 'sands in the morning, donkeys at noon, pier in the afternoon and library at night.' The library was not so impressive or so literary as it sounds. It was a mixture of Casino and Concert Hall, offering games of chance and a party of entertainers whose repertory included comic songs and airs on the guitar. A century has expanded in quantity and not altered in kind the pleasures of a seaside holiday. Here again the heart of England is publicly and blissfully displayed upon the maritime sleeve.

The seaside town must have its pier. The pier, used for fun, is an oddity of English taste which has found expression in a weird splendour of Oriental knobs and garish decoration. When the Prince Regent imposed on Brighton a mad mixture of cupolas and chinoiserie, his Pavilion offered a suggestion for Pier Pavilions up and down the land. Brighton first set a simpler note with its Old Chain Pier, able to withstand many storms but yielding in 1896 to the larger luxury of the present Palace Pier (14). Southend made a magnificent gesture by building a Pier which is more than a mile long. The Bournemouth Pier was launched in 1861 with a bottle of wine, twenty-one guns, and abundant fireworks. Blackpool, never to be outdone, proceeded to equip itself with three Piers, and five Pier Pavilions. Soon every seaside town began to consider itself disgraced without its man-made promontory where lovers could stroll in the moonlight, where bands played and pierrots sang amid the cupolas, where little pleasure steamers came fussing in with strenuous invitation, 'Any more for the Channel trip?' One marvels how the thin metal legs of these strange centipedes can withstand the winter storms; but endure they do. And every summer they provide ample bliss at twopence a head. On the Pier age slumbers in the sun, youth dances or dallies in a gallery of cunning slot-machines, and childhood patiently pursues the small fry of the sea with line and sinker.   Piers, architecturally absurd excrescences from the Marine Parade, are happy places; their lamp-lit platforms end in lovers' meeting.

Happy too are the lodging-houses, at least in the holiday months. Bleak House they may externally seem. But every August they are the gateways and coverlets of young adventure. They are the legacy of Victorian solemnity and spaciousness; huge rooms with huge mahogany sideboards receive the families when school is over. Some still retain the splendour of 'the cruet,' for which a special 'extra' once was charged, a hydra-headed table-monster as grandiose as the great Georgian sauce-cabinet so nobly called 'The Magazine of Taste.' There is a huge hall behind the front-door with its frosted glass and here accumulates a vast clutter of spades, buckets, bathing-dresses, damp towels thick with sand, toy-boats, and the long strips of seaweed which children collect as toy barometers. The landlady frowns at the mess, but puts up with it. At midday there is a powerful odour of roasted mutton and of boiling cabbage; at tea-time the mahogany cupboard yields seed-cake and potted shrimps. So the middle-class family camps for its fortnight or its month according to its purse; here it waits, with strained tempers, for the rain to stop; from this base it sallies forth, when the sun returns, to Pier and Pierrot, to lounge or play indifferent tennis on the public courts, to dig, to paddle, or to bathe. The rents of rooms run very high in the holiday season; in the winter the landlady strives hard to find 'a permanent' and offers lonely ladies the run of her mahogany and the dubious pleasures of her cuisine at bargain-prices.

Nowadays the seaside town inevitably equips itself with a Lido. Why the sands of the Adriatic should supply an inevitable title to all English bathing-pools is a mystery; but, since cinemas are so often called the Capitol or the Rialto, we have come to accept our terminology of Pleasure Domes from alien quarters. Swimming, as a sport, was long suspiciously regarded in England. Sir Nicholas Grimcrack, in a comedy of Shadwell's, used to practise the art in terrestrial safety, stretched, frog-like, on a table. 'I hate the water,' he said. 'I never come upon the water. I content myself with the Speculative part of swimming. I care not for the Practick.' But we have altered all that. If there is sea, we must enter it. If there is no sea, we make a pool and call it a Lido. The Road House of contemporary England is always pool-provided, a paradise for Wet Bobs in the garden, while the Dry Bobs slake a thirst in Ye Olde Tudor Lounge.

Sea-bathing was increasingly favoured in the eighteenth century. It was bravely faced (by practitioners less used to water than ourselves) in the interests of health. A letter written from Scarborough in the early part of the century announces

"It is the Custome, for not only the gentlemen but the ladies also, to bath in the Sea; the gentlemen go out a little way to Sea in Boats (call'd here Cobbles) and jump in naked directly. The Ladies have the Conveniency of Gowns and Guides. There are two little Houses on the Shore, to retire to for Dressing in."

Later on, there were twenty-six bathing machines; but "the Practick" was now a ceremonial and needed equipage. "Two women attend each lady who bathes, as guides; and one man every gentleman who requires it."

The Bathing Machine was one of the great vehicles of the nineteenth century. Now it can be seen shelved on the shingle, mouldering to decay, like the Martello Towers of the old defences, unwanted by a Lido-haunting generation. One had great days in it, queueing up for a tenancy, paying one's tanner, scrambling up the rickety steps, and waiting for the felicitous moment

16 " COME UNTO THESE YELLOW SANDS" : A Wakes-week at Blackpool

17　SOUTHEND IN SUMMER: The Happy Shore

when the patient nag would be harnessed to its frontal shafts and the lumbering cavalcade would go lurching forward into a foot or two of water. They were shabby, sandy, grubby boxes, with broken mirrors on the walls, old hairpins on the floor, and embarrassing advertisements of insecticides for light reading. But in them we were delirious passengers. In them the ladies cumbrously enrobed themselves to preserve the decencies, when they pursued the 'Practick' of immersion. Now the ladies stretch themselves to sun-bathe on the luxurious terraces of the new Lido, which the go-ahead Town Council has implanted on the Esplanade with lavish accoutrements of diving-board and raft and marine café. Our fathers were riders to the natural sea; we summon it to a lake of artifice.

Artifice may be total in the creation of a seaside town. Blackpool was a one-street village of the Fylde when Victoria came to the throne. Now it is England's capital of Pleasure, a marine metropolis, which absorbs the holiday-hungry crowds not of Lancashire only but of all the North and even of the Midlands and the South (16). Here is no history in strips. The town did not grow organically but is a terrific mechanical contrivance for the supply of pleasure. The sand-dunes have been abolished; miles of concrete replace them. Are cliffs essential to the seaside? Very well then, Blackpool will have cliffs, made to measure; it faces the old dunes with imported rock and carefully arranges its cliff-scenery to suit the needs of niche-desirous lovers. Do people want to be mariners without risk of fatality? Of course, so Blackpool walls off the hazardous sea and creates boating-lakes with a secure flotilla and a guaran-

teed depth (or rather shallowness) of eighteen inches.
Blackpool has no purpose but to attract and satisfy and
it does both to the complete approval of democracy. It
is the place in England which most strives to make you
feel that you are wanted. Everywhere there is welcome
and value for money. The latter, of course, is an important factor in Blackpool's success. The prices are marked
and the prices are cheap. Luncheon 2s. 6d. Luncheon 2s.
Luncheon 1s. 6d. Luncheon 1s. Whichever you take, you
get a full whack. There is no place where you are less
likely to be swindled. Everything is good of its kind,
good, that is, for the likely plebeian customer, not for
frowning aesthetes and fussy gourmets. Everything,
except cost, is gigantic. You enter a saloon-bar and
you discover that it stretches for a quarter of a mile.
In the Tower Ball Room on a Saturday night it is as
though all England were dancing. The Fun Fair is
gigantic. The Pierrot shows are gigantic. Should you sit
down to eat, the helpings are gigantic. Blackpool, without a single advantage of natural scenery, has set out
to make itself saleable and then to sell itself. It is an
honest-to-goodness proposition, the bargain-counter of
the holiday emporium, where the trade is terrific because
the bargains are genuine.

So the English seaside town, like the English seaport,
suffers vicissitudes and carves its way. There are more ups
than downs. Here it is an historical manuscript scribbled
over by many hands, fascinating to unravel in all its
'period' phases. Here a decayed harbour has become
the flourishing workshop of caterers and concert-
parties. Here we establish Fifth-Georgian Lidos on the
site of Fourth-Georgian promenades. The old Assembly

Rooms, scene of the silken rally and intemperate rout, have become the new Cinema-Café where the fires of Hollywood passion are discreetly cooled with ice-cream soda. Here again, as at Blackpool, we have started afresh and made a concrete Babylon from a desert of 'bents' and sand. The contribution of the seaside town, new or old, to English health and happiness is enormous. Here every summer, and, in a lesser degree, at Christmas and Easter too, the heart of England, beating warm and sound, is worn bravely on England's blue and pleasant sleeve.

CHAPTER III

THE DOWNS AND THE MOORS

BEHIND the harbour and the seaside town, except upon the level eastern shore below the Humber, a common feature of the English scene is the upward tilt of the land to the downs and the moors; sometimes the ascent is abrupt, downland grass and moorland heath stretching to a sheer boundary of precipitous cliff. Here, since neither is cultivated in its higher reaches, we meet unchanging England. From the plains forests have vanished, scrub has been cleared, and swamps have been drained. To call the ordinary lowland scene 'Nature' is a complete misnomer; fields are things made with hands, wrested from Nature by long labours of hacking and hewing, by the rooting up of stone and weed, ferocious toil; first arduously wrested, then, with no less ardour and endurance, retained. There is nothing less natural than a field of corn, its hedges trim, its crop unwasted by devouring tares. A farm is the assertion of man's victory over nature, a triumph of perspiring artifice. And nowhere does one feel this more keenly than on the edge of the moors, whose dalesmen, seeking pasture for cattle, have through centuries fought their way up the fell-sides, driving back the heather, building walls with the stones torn from the earth, and sometimes abandoning in despair the task of inducing grass to grow and to remain where heather is the natural crop. The verge of moorland and of down has been a perennial battlefield between the obstinate peasant and still more obstinate

18　A MOORLAND FARM IN YORKSHIRE

19 SHEEP AND SNOW IN THE PENNINES

soil; forward and backward and forward again the soil-hungry man has swayed in this earth-grapple of the ages.

As far as landscape is concerned, the hill-country alone can offer us any notion of that England which the ancient mariners colonised, the Celts overran, and the Romans so masterfully swept into their imperial system. When the Archaic men came they lived mainly on the downlands because these alone were habitable without infinities of axe-work; here flints were easily found; their roads were ridgeways because here the track was natural and easy to improve; below lay thicket and marsh. At one time the woodland must have climbed far higher than it does now, as is shown by the timber in the moorland peat. At Tan Hill in the northern tip of Yorkshire, in a wilderness of heather nearly 1,800 feet above the sea, there is coal to be got (and many cheap tons have been got) by scratching at the surface of the moor; timber once grew where now there is no vestige of a tree, nothing but the heather and the moorland grass and the outcrops of bare stone. But the primeval England which made the coal-measures need not trouble us; the England which uses them is more to our purpose. At any rate, if you want to think yourself back into the birth of any English life that can be called civilised, you must go to the hills. Here only can you touch the heart of the matter. Heather on granite or grass on limestone are the old everlastings of our national being; here are the tracks and the testament of the first settlers; here are their barrows, their avenues and circles of stone, their haunts of worship and assembly, their quarryings and delvings, all the relics, often imposing, of a culture which probably was peaceable and certainly had a high degree of calculation and of organising power. Here, too, do some Englishmen still maintain a way of life which has altered less than any other.

The sheep-farmer's and the shepherd's life are nearer to the primitive than all other modes of living in our time. Your prosperous sheep-farmer may now go to market in his motor-car and there is wireless in the home, which breaks down even the isolation of the old Pennine steadings, situated miles apart and fifteen hundred feet or more above sea-level in the rolling desolation of the moorland wastes (18). But, as far as his work is concerned, he owes nothing to machinery. He drives his flock on to the fells, releases the rams in autumn, fights snow-storms in January, superintends the lambing in the early spring and sees to his wool-clip in the summer (24). During a hard winter he and his shepherds will suffer terrible and sometimes even lethal labour in digging the sheep out of the snow-drifts in which they are buried and in which, fortunately, they can keep alive for long periods. After a Pennine blizzard he may have to begin by digging himself out of his own house, round which the snow has piled itself as high as the bedroom windows. Despite wireless and motor-car (and not all possess the latter) the sheep-farmer of the northern moors endures intense loneliness, which might seem inconsiderable to an American or Canadian rancher, who counts miles by the hundred where we count in tens, but is a rare experience for an Englishman. The names of such farms often proclaim a mournful and valedictory note. One such I know called simply 'Farewell.' Candour goes to these titles, a candour far removed from that suburban optimism which finds 'Bella Vista' at the end of a tram-line. Such epithets as 'black' and 'cold' are often included in the name. There is no evasion of the fact.

The northern farmer is generally supposed to be a tough individualist and so in many respects he is; but he can co-operate. The summer 'clip' (24) involves exchange of labour and of subsequent festivity. The men are lent from farm to farm, so that there is always a team which can clip a thousand sheep or more before nightfall. One July day they will all arrive soon after daybreak at Cold Corner, which may, in July, be all too warm a spot for a fifteen-hour stretch of clipping. A few days later the same men will all be at Black Loups. (The word 'Loups' reminds us that wolves lingered late upon this sky-flung wilderness.) The sheep have been rounded up over miles of moorland on previous days and are now pro-pelled in dozens to the dozen of clippers, who deftly yank them on to stools, legs up, and with astonishing neatness and gentleness remove the cumbrous pelt of a year's growth in a few minutes and in a single piece. They can tackle eight or so to the hour and they will stick to it all day long. The sheep do not struggle as a rule; it is July and they are glad to be rid of an encumbrance. There is a midday break for roast beef and suet-pudding, a pause for tea, and then, at night, with a thousand fleeces stacked, the fun begins. The owner of Cold Corner has laid in whisky by the bottle and beer by the barrel and the cards are on the table for nap and pontoon. Thirsts are royally slaked and the hard-earned pennies fly. The clippers do not go home till morning and it is a long tramp when they do. But, if heads are heavy, legs are tough; and some may get a lift.

E

This labour of the sheep-farm is immutable; machinery is irrelevant; it is all muscle and craft, weather-lore and knowledge of the beasts and of the fells. But far too mutable is the price of wool, which has varied in a few recent years from over a shilling a pound to under three-pence. At the latter price it would not be worth clipping, save that the sheep must be relieved of their overcoats. Many sheep-farmers are (or were) wealthy; they have small chance of spending, stick to their Cold Corners, make no rash investments and are expected at death 'to cut up for a packet.' Sometimes they do. Their lives are bleak and may be punctuated by a market-day orgy. But now the wireless has made an enormous difference to their knowledge of the distant world. I remember attending a sheep-clip on a most desolate Pennine farm; I thought that I had mastered the local dialect but, when we sat down to dinner before a joint of beef so large that I could imagine no oven to contain it, the talk was 'broad' beyond my utmost efforts at comprehension. A magnificent veteran, sitting in his shirt-sleeves with a rusty bowler on the back of his head, carved slices a foot long. Here were the English primitives, moormen descended from generations of moormen, speaking their own tongue, untouched by the prim correctness of B.B.C. English. Then one of the incomprehensibles rose from his piled plate and pressed a knob. The room was flooded with jazz, 'hot numbers' from a city café. 'Progress' does somehow penetrate.

In a valuable history and survey of a moorland parish, Kirby Malhamdale, Yorkshire, Mr. J. W. Morkill has tabulated the sheep-scoring numerals in use upon the English mountains. The curious thing is their proximity

20   A COTSWOLD FLOCK

21 DANEWAY, A Cotswold Manor-house

22 THE WHITE HORSE

to the classical words. 'Pimp' for five and 'Dic' for ten are almost pure Greek. 'Teddera' for three and 'Peddera' or 'Methera' for four seem to be a confusion of the Greek 'Tettera.' 'Overa' bears more relation to 'octo' than to 'eight.' 'Tigit' is like a mixture of 'viginti' and 'twenty.' Are these words, with their Grecian echoes, a legacy of the Mediterraneam colonists who preceded the Celt upon the English hills? To what extent are they a relic of the Roman, many of whose auxiliaries were Greek-speakers? The words themselves vary considerably from dale to dale. Seven in Wharfedale is 'Sethera,' in Nidderdale 'Tayter,' in Wensleydale 'Hither' and in the Lake District 'Sethera' once more. The Latin and Greek for seven are 'septem' and 'hepta.'

The tapestry of English history has been largely woven of English wool, a staple which has dictated policy, enriched the herdsman while it impoverished the tiller of the soil and adorned our countryside with noble houses built by the prosperous woolmen when the English fleece was golden and English gold bought beauty. The sheep are graven proudly on their tombs in the churches which wool prosperity endowed. The loveliness of the Cotswold manors (21) was a gift of the Cotswold flocks; the money came when English architecture was in flower. Whenever one sees a Tudor or Jacobean beauty on the edge of moor or down, it is only just to remember the sheep who paid for the craftsmen. On the Woolsack stills sits the Lord Chancellor; out of the woolsack came the Burfords and the Chipping Camdens and many a country town that still is like a lyric writ in stone.

But the sheep, which promoted some men to glorious

estate, consumed the others. The sheep was the agricultural revolutionist of the sixteenth century, when the English pastures swallowed up the English village and left the cultivator a landless and a starving man. The profits of grazing tempted land-owners to an infamous campaign of enclosure. 'Where twenty tillers of the soil had once been employed a single shepherd now sufficed and shepherds were the worst paid of all classes of rural labourers.' Thus Professor Lipson in his *Economic History of England*, and the rhymes and pamphlets of Tudor England ring with denunciation of the cannibal sheep. "Sheep have become devourers of men," cried Sir Thomas More. The engrossing of farms, the joining of field to field, the substitution of grass for corn, had devastating results. "Enclosures make fat beasts and lean people" was a popular proverb and

'Sheep have eaten up our meadows and our downs,
Our corn, our woods, whole villages and towns.'

But, as far as our present subject is concerned, the grazier's quest of new wealth did far less damage. For the moors and the downs cannot be corn-land, at least on their higher reaches. The sheep had long been native there; it was their descent upon the valleys, coupled with the increasing collapse of the medieval economy and the arrival of commercial buccaneering, that turned them into eaters of men. Never were more guiltless assassins; bleating songs of innocence they came.

The English hills have yielded other harvest than fleece and mutton. They have provided us with stone and slate, with iron and lead. Their caves housed the

true Primitives of the first Stone Age and their flints
gave tools to the settlers of the Second, whose miners,
working with antler-picks, ran their galleries into the
Sussex downs or Yorkshire wolds. The later quarrymen
have carved deep into the face of some noble ridges,
chipping the sharp Malvern spine and wellnigh decapi-
tating one of the Shropshire Clees. Often the stone of
the level counties or of the shore, notably of the Lincolnshire and Midland oolite and of the Portland promontory,
have contributed nobly to English building. Out of
Lincolnshire came many of the Cambridge Colleges;
out of the Cotswolds St. John's and Christ Church at
Oxford. Southward the quarries near Bath offered one
of the most popular of English stones. Mr. A. K. Wick-
ham in his book on the villages of England has com-
mented on the golden tinge which the quarries of Ham
Hill have bestowed on Sherborne Abbey and the
towers of many Somerset churches. Finally, there is the
monarch of all English stones, Portland, brought to
London by Inigo Jones for the Banqueting Hall and
then approved by Sir Christopher Wren, who married
his genius to its mighty, shimmering blocks and so begat
St. Paul's and many region spires. If Lincolnshire made
Cambridge, Dorset made the City. The first and perfect
praise of Portland Stone has been written by Mr. James
Bone in his full, affectionate study of the subject in
The London Perambulator.

'No poet has sung of Portland stone, although great ones
have sung of sofas and mice and marine engines. Yet it is a
great and magical stone, more beautiful, I think, even than
the Roman travertine, with its marmoreal quality that responds
so exquisitely to wear. Portland stone seemed ordained to

form the face of London, its surface so finely mirroring the fitful lights . . . . that break through her river-mists, blanching in her towers and spires to a finer whiteness as the darker grow the coats of grime at the bases and sides. How those towers and spires come and go through the mists as you watch from Waterloo Bridge over the grey-blue Thames on a spring morning! Who can ever forget his first vision of it all as he beheld, round the bend of the river, the apparition of the mighty fleet of Wren, with their top-gallants and mainsails of stone?'

Certainly no book upon the heart of England could ignore the stone that we have riven from her flesh. The subject is too vast for more than a salute in such an essay as this. But the salute is none the less a sincere obeisance to the quarries and the men of the quarries who made English architecture possible.

Those who tramp the northern moors will continually find holes in them, mere pock-marks on the great, tough Pennine skin, deserted delvings, often surmounted by a ruined shack of stone or the tumbled elements of a miners' village with its smelting mills. The wind blows through their raggedness; no more shafts are driven, no more mountain ponies remove the mineral load. They are nothing now, but once the workshops of a great lead industry, whose roots are in pre-history. The Mediterranean colonists busily sought out and exploited the English deposits, and their megalithic remains are commonly situate in the midst of their metal hunting-grounds. Megaliths are as richly mingled with Cornish tin and Derbyshire lead as with the flints of Dorset and of Wiltshire. Arbor Low, the Avebury of the North, is in the heart of the lead-bearing Derbyshire plateau, and the long barrows of the Archaic men are

23　THE QUARRY

24　THE CLIP

25   GROUSE-SHOOTING ON A NORTHERN MOOR

set about that region. These delving adventurers could not operate with iron; the iron deposits of the Cleveland Hills were for a later age to cultivate. But where there is lead there are the signs and rumours of a rare antiquity; the signs are the standing stones—'standards' as they call them in the Pennine country—and the rumours are of far-off commerce with the East. One of the richest lead-bearing districts was Arkengarthdale, a tributary of Swaledale in North Yorkshire. There is an old rhyme of that district.

> 'When Julius Caesar was a king
> Bowes Castle and Hurst and Arkendale
> Mines was a famous thing.'

Such popular jingles and local rumour are often of great historical value. If 'Arkendale' was not a 'famous thing' in Roman times, why should anyone imagine it?

Bowes had a Roman camp (the ruins of the bath are still visible beside the Norman castle), and in Wensleydale there is direct evidence to confirm the common tradition of Roman working of the Yorkshire lead. Mr. W. Riley in *The Yorkshire Pennines of the North West* quotes a Swaledale story that Swaledale lead was exported before the Roman came and went to roof the buildings in Jerusalem. For a fuller picture of the time when lead meant gold to the Pennines Miss Ella Pontefract's book on *Swaledale*, an admirable piece of regional research, is of great value.

So the moorlands yielded a harvest and made money. One Yorkshire lead-mine alone yielded a profit of £60,000 in a year. Our English churches were roofed from the Pennine moors, themselves the natural roof of England. What Lincoln built, Yorkshire capped. The fell-sides, whose only inhabitants now are the sheep and the grouse, had busy colonies of miners; many of the workings were financially unified and administered by the 'Great Corporation for smelting down lead with Pitt Coale and Sea Coale' which received a charter during the reign of William and Mary and did not dissolve until 1911. The lead industry collapsed, mainly from the pressure of Spanish imports towards the end of the nineteenth century. There is still some lead-getting in the Derbyshire end of the Pennine Chain, but elsewhere the pursuit of native veins has proved too costly to withstand the foreign competition. The moors once afforded great wealth to the owners of the land in royalties on lead and a rough, dangerous, but not un-profitable living to the miners. According to Mr. H. W. Bainbridge, a Teesdale man brought up amid great mining traditions, the Great Corporation was a good employer, provided education for the child as well as work for the parent and carried its workers through patches of bad luck when a new-tapped vein proved sterile. All that is left now is the skeleton-cottage in the heather, the hole in the ground, and sometimes the shell of an old smelting-mill, carefully and exquisitely fashioned at a time when builders cared as much for beauty as for durability.

Over these ghosts of old prosperity and débris of an English industry that flourished before the Roman came, the winds blow bleak as the names of the old moorland mines. What a harsh, queer music and what strange suggestion do these names contain! By the Arkle Beck alone you will find Whaw and Booze and Racca Vein;

26 HIKERS IN A DERBYSHIRE DALE

27 PITMEN

28 GUN-MEN

what tragedy befell Windegg? What merriment came to Jingle-pot? Mr. Bainbridge in a glorious list of 'Corporation' mines cites Dowpotsike, Rampgill, Coldberry, Lady's Rake, Flushamie and Cowslitts. Down the winds the grouse go sailing, in late summer to their fate. The moorlands are still the pasture of the mountain sheep, yielding a good coarse wool but mutton only after fattening on the lower levels. They are no longer a mine-field and a workshop; but they are, like the downs, increasingly a playground. For their noble spaces there is sometimes bitter strife, between the owner of shooting rights and the claimants of walking rights. This conflict has become especially acute at the southern end of the Pennines, where the industrial towns run right into the coveted heather. The issue is less urgent further north, because there are no great populations to spill their 'hikers' on the hills and also because the moors are themselves more spacious. I have never been interrupted by a gamekeeper in the grand stretch of country between Wensleydale and Tees, over which I have walked a good deal; it is advisable to keep to the tracks across the fells, if only because the moors themselves make such heavy going; one soon tires of walking knee-deep in heather and dodging the 'mosses' or bogs.

The Peak District, that wild barrier between the huge populations of S.E. Lancashire and S.W. Yorkshire, has offered particular occasions for dispute, especially during the last ten years when 'hiking' has been so popular with the youth of the towns. Certainly the case for the 'Access to Mountains Bill' is here most strongly supported by the facts. The Enclosures of the early nineteenth century drove the public from many ancient

F

moorland tracks in the interests of land-owners for whom the grouse are a highly profitable investment. Derbyshire abounds in wild beauty denied to the public and none of its major 'downfalls,' as waterfalls are there called, is visitable by the tramper on the hills. Mr. P. A. Barnes, a vigorous champion of walkers' rights, thus summarises the situation.

'Although Bleaklow is only sixteen miles in a straight line from the centres of Manchester or Sheffield, there are surrounding this ridge thirty-seven square miles of wild country quite unknown except to the few ramblers who defy these unjust restrictions and take the access so far denied to them by the law. Similarly to the east of the Derwent reservoirs there are the extensive Broomhead, Howden and Derwent moorlands, in all covering thirty-two square miles, with only three undisputed public ways across them. Whilst Kinderscout, affording in many ways the most exhilarating and picturesque scenery in the district, is very strictly preserved. Here are fifteen square miles of mountainous country with no public path. . . . Through the moorland area in and adjacent to the Peak District (about 215 square miles) there are, as a matter of fact, only twelve footpaths across moorland which exceed two miles in length. The rest are mainly short paths near the fringe of the moors.'

On the southern moors of Dart and Exe there is far less interference with walkers because, fortunately for the South, the grouse will not flourish below the Midlands. Here, for the most part, one can wander at will, watching on Dartmoor the moorland ponies enjoy their brief freedom or keeping an Exmoor eye for a possible glimpse of the red deer there preserved, not for charity's sake, but that horse and hound may pursue them in due course. The Exmoor conflict is not so much of walker against shooter, as of humanitarian against hunter. On this issue feeling runs high in North Devon. The downs are nearly always open to walkers; their grass feeds little 'game' and the enemy here is the barbarian who will drive motor-car and motor-cycle across the turf, bringing noise and fumes to the flowered ridgeways of the Sussex and the Wiltshire chalk.

In August the newspapers are full of 'reports from the moors,' estimating the likely 'bag' of grouse or recording the achievement of a record slaughter. The grouse, which abound upon the Pennine heather, have made an industry. It is true that, if they were not 'kept down' by shooting, they would overpopulate their territory and suffer ravages of disease. But that is owing to the sportsman's greedy interference with the balance of Nature. In order to stock the moors with the maximum number of grouse, his keepers have trapped and shot every possible bird and beast that could thin the coveys. The northern fells should have their eagles and the lesser raptorial birds; the names tell the tale of these soaring beauties; Raven Crags abound; there are Buzzard Mosses and Falcon Clints (a 'clint' is an abrupt piece of rock projecting from the moor). But there are no ravens or buzzards or falcons; not a kestrel even may escape for long. That keeper who allowed any such to hover or swoop above his native wilds would be workless in a week.

Shooting has long been a popular pastime of the English country gentleman and preservation of the game-birds was strict. One remembers the sad encounter of young Tom Jones with Mr. Allworthy's sporting neighbour, of whom Fielding ironically remarked,

'This species of men, from the great severity with which they revenge the death of a hare or partridge, might be thought to cultivate the same superstition with the Bannians in India; many of whom, we are told, dedicate their whole lives to the preservation and protection of certain animals; was it not that our English Bannians, while they preserve them from other enemies, will most unmercifully slaughter whole horse-loads themselves; so that they stand acquitted of any such heathenish superstition.'

But the gunners of Fielding's time were roughly equipped with the flint-lock; the amount of shooting was limited by the labours of loading and the slow ignition. Even had Messrs. Winkle & Tupman brought uncanny skill to their famous expedition, they could not have rivalled the 'bag' of a modern shooting party. The great days of shooting were to come in the second half of the nineteenth century, when the breech-loader was introduced and followed by the mechanical perfection of the hammerless two-barrel gun with automatic ejection of the cartridges. A shooter, equipped with several such weapons and a servant to keep handing him a new-loaded implement as the driven birds come pelting past, has the destructive power of a machine-gun. It needs a quick eye and a hand as sure as swift (some of the most brilliant shots have been Indian grandees, like 'Ranji,' as miraculous with a gun as with a cricket bat); but nowa-days it demands nothing but these qualities and money in the purse. The shooters are not tested in wind and limb, since they arrive in their motor-cars almost at the butts; the old ardours of 'walking-up' birds through the heather, which was gruelling exercise, have been abandoned for the more sedentary pleasures of the shooting-stick on which a perched sportsman waits for the game to be driven to him.

The keeping of the moors, the loading of guns and the beating-up of the birds have created a late summer occupation for the descendants of the old lead-miners and for the sheep-farmers' men who have finished the hay-harvest and the clipping of the sheep. A good Pennine moor, like Bowes or Blubberhouses or Wemmergill, famous for their record 'bags,' may bring a rental of thousands of pounds for a season (25). It is a rich man's pleasure. First divide the rental by the number of days on which shooting takes place; then allow for a dozen beaters at seven-and-sixpence with a solid lunch; then throw in the wage of loaders (ten shillings each day) and of keepers, maintenance of dogs, expenditure on cartridges and tips on a lavish scale and it is easy to realise that the sportsmen of a fashionable moor are paying a guinea a brace for their birds. So you may estimate the cost of a 'record' day when seven or eight 'guns' will account for thousands of the birds. The Peak District record is 2,843 birds shot by nine guns on the Broomhead moors in 1913.

Undoubtedly those who scatter pellets scatter money too. But happier for the community are the grass-covered hills of the Lake District, the green downs and wolds and the grouseless heather of the South. The downland offers infinite scope to the horseman, whether he be the professional trainer of pedigree stock for the racecourse or the humble tenant of a hired hack. Riding has recently become cheaper and more popular and the downs are much frequented by the casual cavalry of the week-end. The heather makes too heavy and dangerous going and it is the walker who most frequents the northern moors, or such as he can traverse without risk of prosecution. That a few passers-by amid vast spaces would do any harm to the shooting is debatable and the Access to Mountains Bill, which has been intermittently before the House of Commons since 1888, specifically excludes from its protection of the recreational walker all persons going in pursuit of game or wild birds; also those taking eggs, bringing dogs or carrying fire-arms, camping, lighting fires, damaging trees, buildings and fences, removing plants, or disturbing flocks. It seems to be an innocent measure, rendered increasingly politic by the increasing passion for pedestrian exercise. Motor-cars have made the roads hateful and hazardous to walkers and in the industrial towns of the Pennines, if the moors are barred, there is small scope for rambling else-where. They are, as we have pointed out, the scenes of age-long habitation and of industry, essential heart of England. Here are emptiness, silence and, above all, distance; are they to be legally endowed with so extreme a solitude that none but the owner and the tenant-shooters can enjoy their loneliness?

of Clare Leighton

COUNTRY MATTERS

At the foot of the downs and the moors is the village (29). In praise of the English Village so much has been said, and with such lavishness of sentiment, that further ecstatic essays on the rose-clad porches and the ivied cots are certainly not wanted. As for the aspect, one may say that the English village has often been extremely lucky. It was not planned, but it came right. Frequently one notices, especially in the case of a village which climbs a hill, that the lines of the walls and roofs ride beautifully with the lines of the land. A genius, taking thought could not have patterned it better; there is no greedy, vulgar perching on hill-tops; the early villagers did not want 'views'; they wanted shelter and they wanted water, whereas the modern week-ender, building a little country place, loves to possess a prospect. Accordingly he pitches on a summit and his prickly villa probably gashes the sky-line. The villagers, not wanting 'views,' created one; the new arrival, seeking 'a view,' destroys it—at least for other people.

The picturesque façade of the traditional English cottage is usually the mask of a rural slum. The cottage is dark and damp, short of windows, totally deficient in sanitation. The water may have to be fetched from a pump. The accommodation is utterly inadequate for a family of any size. The rents obtainable from rural workers are so small that the landlord cannot recondition these places without serious loss; often no blame attaches to the owner, who may be quite a poor man, quite unable to sustain a large outlay. On the other hand, I know of some rich men, praised for 'preserving villages' and 'keeping up the district,' who were really behaving in a most anti-social way by refusing to build new cottages for the villagers, while they profitably sold sites for good houses to wealthy week-enders. In some villages even the worst hovels are eagerly sought. After the war some efforts had to be made to remedy the appalling shortage of accommodation in villages as in towns; most villages, accordingly, received a row of 'Council Houses' (30). Sometimes these are abominably ugly, made of material and roofed with a covering which are quite alien to the rest of the cottages; brick and tile villages have been defaced with concrete and slate additions. Occasionally, however, the job has been decently done by trained architects instead of being rushed through by a jerry-builder. Then utility is served without affront to the amenities.

In the centre of the village is the village inn (32) and here again the rhapsodists have cried themselves hoarse with jubilation, finding the stout heart of England beating in the rural 'pub.' But a great many village inns are tawdry beer-houses, where an incompetent landlord 'tied' to an indifferent brewery, serves out tepid swipes in dirty glasses in a fly-blown bar whose walls are hung with the less attractive specimens of drink-trade advertisements. If you call at midday and ask for food, the chances are that you meet a sullen face, some stale bread and the kind of rank, imported cheese which is just about good enough for baiting mice. Of course there are many lovely village inns and some of them are competently

29 POYNINGS, SUSSEX, at the foot of the South Downs

30 OLD MILL AND COUNCIL HOUSES : A Cambridgeshire Contrast

31 THE APPLE MARKET

kept; the reader has only to consult Professor Richardson's admirable book on *The Old Inns of England* to realise their beauty and to mark their names for future visitation. But I am considering the average small agricultural village possessing no especial 'tourist' value. Should a wayfarer happen to wander in, heated perhaps and thirsty or chilled by a nipping air and with a roaring hunger, could anybody fairly guarantee his chances of an encouraging welcome and of satisfactory service for all his needs? There is sure to be one cottage in the village with the familiar placard 'Teas,' and you may rely on finding here substantial bread, butter and jam, and lumps of home-made cake, no stuff for city appetites and motorists' digestions, but consoling and assimilable after a day's walking on the hill-tops.

It can hardly be said that the English inn has 'gone down'; it was never 'up.' More romantic rubbish has been written about 'mine hoste' of the good old days than on any other topic in English life. The chief halts on the main coaching routes, usually in towns rather than in villages, maintained a comfortable flow of hot brandy-and-water for resuscitation of the half-frozen bodies that tumbled off the coach's roof. There would be hot joints, steaming punches and blazing fires; there had to be, for the numbed traveller would have perished otherwise. But investigation into the travel-records of the seventeenth and eighteenth centuries reveals some fearful stories of dirty rooms and bad feeding off the principal roads. Justices were continually pursuing the keepers of ale-houses for refusing entertainment, and John Taylor, the Water Poet who travelled the West of England in 1649, was driven from

G

two taverns and six ale-houses in Cornwall without room or refreshment, and in Somerset he found an inn where

'the Hostesse was out of Towne, mine Host was very sufficiently drunke, the house most delicately deckt with exquisite artificiall and natural sluttery, the roome besprinkled and strewed with the Excrements of Pigs and Children; the walls and ceilings were adorned and hanged with rare Spider's Tapestry, or Cobweb Lawne; the smoake was so palpable and perspicuous, that I could scarce see anything else.'

Here he was promised food and got none. At last, having purchased bread and butter, he went to bed and killed five hundred fleas of the fattest. He further adds,

'For my further delight, my chamber-pot seemed to be lined with crimson plush, or shag'd scarlet bayes, it had escaped a scouring time out of minde, it was fur'd with antiquity and withal it had a monumental savour; and this pisse-pot was another of my best contentments.'

Celia Fiennes, a great seventeenth-century traveller, complained bitterly of the ale-houses where accommodation and manners were bad and refreshment worse. 'Mine hoste,' with the apple-cheeks, the quenchless smile, the spotless linen, the great spread of joints and sweets, the shining pewter and the noble cheese was perchance to be discovered in the centre of a market town or on a coaching route. But from the ordinary village he was absent and still is.

The village publican has his excuses. Nobody trained him. He drifted into his job. He is a brewers' employee and has no capital of his own. Less than a penny per pint of beer sold is small allowance for 'over-heads' in a small village where incomes are equally diminutive.

32 THE WAY TO THE WEST AT WYLYE, WILTSHIRE

33   THE THRESHERS

34   "MINE'S A BITTER"

It was not so bad just after the war when the agricultural wages were up to forty shillings or more; but, when they fell back to twenty-eight, the beer-money dwindled and almost disappeared. One village publican told me that his weekly sale fell in a year or two from a hundred and twenty gallons to less than thirty. And catering for week-end walkers and motorists is such a risky business for a poor man to undertake. Stores are laid in, perishable stuff like bread and meat; there comes a day or two of steady rain, nobody arrives and it is all left on the publican's hands. His profit for a fine week-end will not make up for the loss on a wet one. Besides, even in fine weather his luck may be out. People drop in plentifully one Saturday; next time they all pass by. It is a chancy business, hazardous, even ruinous for those who lack capital. Much might be done by the brewery companies, who own nearly all the village 'pubs,' if they would assist, inform, inspect and generally encourage their tenants to be real innkeepers. But their profits are usually so high that they do not bother. Some Trust Companies, local and national, have bought up and improved a number of village, as of urban, inns. The disadvantage of this is the monotony of standardised service, decoration and menu. But the gains are important. The visitor at a 'Trust' house can rely on cleanliness, civility and a reasonable meal at a reasonable price. Naturally the Trusts prefer 'show' houses in 'show' places, but they have reconditioned with care some of the smaller ale-houses and made them into seemly inns with food always available and a landlord who has been educated in his business.

The country inn, good or bad, still serves the purpose

of a forum and a play-room. It is the men's club (34); the women, if they meet socially outside their cottages, generally go to the Institutes which most villages now possess through charity of the 'big houses' or as a War Memorial. The chief public-house games are darts, shove-halfpenny and dominoes and Saturday night provides brisk conflict in all of them. The tap-room is also the scene of clamorous discussion on politics and economics and, perhaps more often, the sins of one's neighbours and the likely winner of a big race. As Mr. G. K. Chesterton has remarked, the English democrat has never been so much interested in the equality of man as in the inequality of horses.

The women of the English village, though they lack the foreigner's capacity to create savoury meals out of almost nothing, are marvels at 'making do.' Probably thirty shillings a week come into the average cottage; on this children are born and reared and clothed, often in embarrassing quantity. Between the intervals of child-birth, there is an endless routine of house-work, washing, mending, sewing; even so, the woman may manage to 'go out' and make a few extra shillings by 'charring' in one of the big houses. How anybody in the village ever has a new pair of shoes is one of the mysteries insoluble by middle-class minds. Yet, miracle of miracles, when the village cricket-team turns out in summer, it will be discovered that 'Dad' can sport a pair of white trousers and even cricket-boots. Dad has a pint or two after the game on Saturday and Ma, one hopes, takes the 'bus to 'the pictures' in the country-town at least now and again; she deserves her glimpse of Hollywood grandeur and the purple passions of the great, if that is her cup of tea. Tea, after all, is the strongest liquor that she ever touches during most weeks in the year. Furthermore purple passions, emerging from exquisite gowns, are more fun than the lecture at the Institute which a high-minded lady at the Grange provides on winter afternoons.

Most of them, too, somehow afford a wireless set. I have heard profound discussion on the merits of 'Charlot's Hour' in a tap-room amid the wildest moors. The village is no longer in isolation. Petrol flows from the parish pump and the farmer's sons have motor-bicycles. I have heard it complained that the village cricket-team is not what it was because the youngsters will not join up; their Saturday afternoons are spent with beauty on the pillion and the Picture-drome to follow. There is a 'bus-service to the nearest town and a special 'bus runs late on Saturday night for those who have had the small silver necessary to make the trip, shop at Woolworth's and end up with Clark Gable, even with fish and chips. There are annual 'outings' in the summer, with a special 'chara' hired and the seaside, if attainable, as destination. There is one outing specially for mothers and another, probably, in which Dad can join. Male or female, one can get a bit 'tiddly' without shame and sing songs on the way home.

One of the perennial festivals of village life is the Show. On the plains it will be a Flower Show; on the hills, where gardens are less generous, the exhibits will be on a larger scale, sheep, cattle and horses. The Flower Show includes bread, cakes and vegetables, everything a cottager can turn out. It happens, probably, on a July Saturday. There is a grand assembly beneath a scorching sun; inside the tents, their tables stacked with tapering carrots, monstrous marrows, giant lettuces and onions which are their cultivators' darlings, the heat is terrific. There is a touch of temper, as well as thunder, in the air. For old Smith, whose onions were put second last year to those of Jones, has fertilised this year's crop with the sweat of infinite contemplation. For the last few weeks the world has been his onions; more exactly, his onions have been his world. He is not going to be bettered this time, not by any man in the country. The judges set about their dreadful office—dreadful for themselves since they are bound to make enemies before the day is out—and the coloured labels are attached to the exhibits. A 'first' for Smith! Justice at last and a pint—more likely a gallon before the night is out—to celebrate the tardy triumph of the Right. And for Jones, too, consoling pints, when the verdict is over and the time has come to talk of many things, including the pride and folly and wickedness of those who sit in judgment.

Meanwhile the Brass Band, from the nearest town, has been lustily rendering *The Gondoliers* and kindred airs. The village flower show is inconceivable without Sullivan. The children have had races, with the parson very hot and red and active as a referee; there have been coconut-shies and buried treasure-hunts and Aunt Sallies; pigs and fowls have been raffled for the Prize Fund; now it is the time for the dancers. The Brass Band, refreshed, plunges, with more good will than good management, into the tunes of the year and aspires to jazz. That achievement limps behind aspiration is no deterrent; the youngsters go to it. This is their Folk Dance, whatever the high-minded lady at the Grange may endeavour to

35 A DEVON CATTLE-MARKET

36 VILLAGE CRICKET IN HAMPSHIRE

teach them about morrises and all such. The village now
is part and parcel of that universe whose melodies
originate from the quick cleverness of Broadway Jews;
it has heard the tunes on the wireless and knows the
rhythms well enough when the Brass Band goes panting
in their pursuit. But among the elders there are some
grievings and resentments. That mighty lettuce fobbed
off with a 'third!' That plum-cake only 'recommended!'
Those raspberries entirely spurned! In Village Shows
there are no fruit without some sourness, no flowers
without thorns.

Most English villages of any size have a football and
a cricket team. The game, in both cases, is played hard.
Village cricket, like the village inn, has been often senti-
mentalised, mostly by people who have never played it.
I have been enticed into the arena and I remember some
hot contentions in the League matches which decided
the year's ownership of the region's Cup. Village sides
are not just jovial sportsmen who want a knock. They
are partisans who play to win and, if the village black-
smith has a knack of 'body-line' bowling, his captain
will not discourage him. The pitch is usually abominable
and, in dry weather, really dangerous, be it farmer's
meadow or village green. Batsmen, however, have no
scruples about departing towards square-leg if that
retreat seems to offer personal security. Umpires have
no escape. They do their best; if perplexed, they give
'leg before' decisions 'in' and 'out' alternately, which
procedure, like Bacon's definition of revenge, is wild
justice, but has its wildness tempered by a sort of equity.
They receive small thanks and many scowls. But to be
the village umpire is an office favoured by the elders and

veterans too stiff for the game. It gives authority; the white coat is a kingly robe. I have known the litigious spirit bitterly aroused in Cup Matches over the exact position of the boundary; two teams were enemies for years over a dispute about a bank of nettles. Did the batsman get six runs for a hit clean over the nettles or clean into the nettles? I forget the decision. But there were angry words and even correspondence; the papers were despatched to some remote Headquarters of the League, which should, like the League of Nations, have sent an International Mixed Commission to investigate the nettles. Perhaps they did go so far as to despatch a panel of arbitrators from Neutral Villages.

But there are friendly matches too; and quarrelling, after all, is part of man's fun on earth. The cricketers enjoy their afternoon and the spectators enjoy it too (36). If the parson isn't in the game himself, he takes a keen interest; the local big-wigs drop in for a few minutes or provide teas for both teams. Passers-by stop to look on; surely nobody ever walked through an English village on a Saturday afternoon without ten minutes' interval beside the cricket-match. Motorists, even motorists in sports cars, who never stop anywhere, unless compelled, draw up by the green. My own observation suggests that village cricket has recently become much more formal; it is unusual to see a fielder in his workaday clothes or a batsman displaying braces and a bowler hat. Flannels are ubiquitous and some villages now have dark blue caps like county teams and sight-screens behind the wickets. The players cannot be as dull as county experts, rather because they lack the time than because they lack the spirit. I have seen some young villagers

37, 38 PASTURE AND PARK

39 AUTUMN MORNING IN THE SHIRES

pottering about the wicket in a terribly professional
manner.

Returning to more serious matters, we may ask what
change there has been in the sovereignty of village life?
Authority long rested in the squire and the parson; to
a less extent in the policeman and the schoolmaster.
The squirearchy is undoubtedly weaker than it was;
when a man sells part of his estate, he sheds some influence. When he sells all and lets a new man in, a new man,
probably, whose interests are mainly urban, he replaces
a native by a visitor; the visitor may hunt and shoot
and fulfil other squirely duties; he may send far bigger
cheques to cottage hospitals and Flower Show funds
than his predecessor ever did; but he does not belong
and his influence is small. The idea of the old landed
gentry as impoverished saints and of the newcomer as
a conscienceless cad, which had some sort of backing
in Galsworthy's novels and plays, is another aspect of
urban sentiment on rustic matters. The old squires often
gave little enough value for their lazy, privileged lives
and the new owner of 'the big house' may repair and
rebuild and take his responsibilities along with his rents
if he can get them. It is not a matter for curt generalisation; but it is fairly obvious that the authority of the
landed gentry has dwindled. Opinion about private
conduct and public affairs now derives more from wireless talks and news, from increased reading of newspapers and from better schooling and much less from
traditional, unquestioned notions of right and wrong.

Yet politically the village remains conservative.
Apart from central business areas and middle-class
suburbs, there are few urban constituencies which

H

Labour cannot hope immediately to capture if the national feeling runs Labour's way. On the other hand there are few purely agricultural areas where it can hope for early victory. Until quite recently there was a strong Liberal vote where the Nonconformist Churches were strong, notably in East Anglia and the far West. The splitting of the party and the diminished appeal of the chapel have weakened that old and really conservative attachment to the Liberal cause. But the defaulters have not gone over, like many of the urban radicals, to Labour. They may be cursed by one side as servile or praised by the other as sturdy, sensible individualists, but it seems that Socialism, as a name, has still its terrors for the country-side. Meanwhile a Conservative Minister of Agriculture is busy socialising that industry to a degree beyond the dreams of radicals; the farm is now State-controlled and State-aided as never before. Life's little ironies begin at home; the larger ironies at Westminster.

The parson is still there, living, perhaps in half of the rectory, closing the rest, pinching, scraping and keeping a respectable air. As the old serene shepherds of a docile flock dwindle and vanish, he tends to be of a new type; he served in the war as chaplain or combatant; he is democratic and wants to make closer, easier contacts with the parish. But, at least in the 'servile south,' the villager is shy of him. In a village which I knew well one of the heartier back-slapping types replaced an old vicar who had kept himself to himself, held his services and gone a tranquil way. The younger man's good intentions and friendly manner were not altogether approved. There was a feeling that parsons should be parsons, functioning on Sundays and available to marry and bury,

40 CHICKEN FARM

41 RIPE FOR HARVEST : A Berkshire Scene

but otherwise decently, discreetly remote. Perhaps that young man has now broken down the tacit resentment of his bright and brotherly manner. He and his kind may become a force in the village life, but the parsonage, on the whole, has been so much an appendage of 'the big house' that a collapse of the squire's influence inevitably affected the parson's too. The secularisation of Sunday— they have taken to playing Sunday Cricket on one village green of my acquaintance—the catering for hikers and week-enders and the presence of the motor-bus to take villagers away on Sunday visits, all work against church-going and the rival attractions of the chapel. So the new parson, being more seen, is less heard.

The village policeman continues to represent the law and, as our laws multiply like rabbits and develop devilish complications, his office becomes more onerous. What with Foot and Mouth Disease, all the new Agricultural Orders, shop hours, the liquor laws, the preservation of birds and birds' eggs and flowers, the technicalities of trespass and the survey of weights and measures, the poor man must be an encyclopaedia as well as a good, burly fellow. In fact, he tends to work more by common sense than by the book; his main duties are nocturnal; he sets out after dark with a bicycle to keep an obligatory 'date' with his colleague of the next police-district. He learns more about nature than man in the process. It is a dull job and 'shiny nights' may invite him to use his dog and his local knowledge. All that I know of poaching was taught me by a country policeman on his official midnight journeys. He had a grand dog, a grand thirst and a grand fund of stories. But, in fairness to the Force, I should add that he was subsequently removed from it and later passed inside the cells which he had helped others to enter. I take it there are few such as my friend and add that he was grand company. The country policeman has a strong dislike for the gipsies so dear to the urban novelist. Raggle-taggle folk have no charms for him; they mean petty theft and complaints and trouble of all sorts. So he edges them, on suspicion, over the county boundary and then the police of the other county edge them back. As a rule the village constable is a popular fellow, executes the law with tact and is no preceptor of morals. They are parson's business.

The schoolmaster of the village has always had, if sensitive, a life of disappointment. He knocked a little knowledge into the children and saw them, at fourteen, depart to predestined ends, the boys to the field, the girls to the kitchen. There was no follow-up, no developing of his rudiments. But now the brighter children go on to County Secondary Schools and may climb the scholarship ladder to the top rungs at the University. Hardy's obscure Jude, had he been born in 1920, might have triumphantly entered the Oxford which repulsed him. It does not happen to many, but the schoolmaster has now more to watch, and more hope of fostering talent to some purpose instead of sending potential scholars away from books to the inevitable byre and stable, the oven and the scrubbing brush.

He is a keener type of man than of old, politically on the Left as a rule, and eager to improve the job of teaching. He voluntarily gives up part of his holidays to attending the Summer Schools on educational method which the Board of Education provides; in the rest of his leisure he travels as far as his scanty means will allow.

His authority in the village has always been indirect;
but, if minds can be formed in an elementary school,
he is probably doing it far better than it was ever done
before. Furthermore, his ex-pupils have more opportunity to realise that all knowledge does not end at fourteen. The Village Institute has a shelf or two of books;
a motor-van brings the travelling section of the County
Library; there is radio in most homes and the Rural
Drama Society instigates play-acting on the little Institute
stage; things of the mind do not peter out as they did
for the village boy and girl. So life has more interest for
the men and women whose often irksome task it is to
stir those minds to first activity.

CHAPTER V

MARKETS AND MILLS

THE dreariest thing in England—and certainly in Scotland and Wales—is the industrialised village; one thinks of the miners' settlements—village and town are names too civil and too honourable for these slums among the slag-heaps, which the Age of Anyhow, as Mr. Baldwin has aptly called it, deemed good enough for the followers of an ancient and dangerous calling. We can claim that, when we start afresh on such a job, as in the Kentish coalfield, we do it better; but we have done little enough to clear up the mess in the older mining counties. The staple of wool built beauty in the seventeenth century; the staple of coal befouled our country in the nineteenth. The courage and endurance of the miner are tested as much when he emerges from the pit as when he enters it. What a place in which to rest and seek the sun!

Sometimes a market-town has accepted mills and factories without loss of its own quality. Macclesfield, so comfortably settled between the severity of the Derbyshire Pennines and the rich pastures of the Cheshire plain, is a case in point. Its silk-mills have mellowness and, when its Saturday market loads the streets with Cheshire cheese, the two kingdoms of the field and the factory seem to be well and truly blended, as they say of other good things such as whisky, tea and tobacco.

The market-town of England has many attractions, not least the attraction of variety. It has often been pointed out that the traveller in America may go a

42   THE ENGLISH HIGH STREET : Dorking, Surrey

43 THE CATHEDRAL CITY : Worcester from the Severn

thousand miles and find himself in something indistinguishable from the place which he has just left. In England assimilation increases with the multiplication of the multiple store, the row of petrol pumps and the monotonous façades of the new cinema and the new garage. But assimilation is of the surface only and that only partial. It is far from absolute. Keswick, and Lewes, Totnes and Barnard Castle, Devizes and Pickering may observe the same Hollywood Venus in the same film on the same day. Yet they have not become the same town. Difference of building and architectural style, of staple products, of dialects, of religious sect and of general mood and tempo remain to fight the unifying forces. Rapid mutability is one of England's eternal fascinations; an hour's run in train or motor-car, perhaps less, will carry you into entirely new surroundings, from down to forest, from sheep to corn, from grass to heather, from hedges to stone walls, from the red mellowness of old brick houses to the grey ripeness of the weathered stone.

The market-town of England may be defined as one very broad street, several very narrow ones and a fine spread of taverns. The broad street, leading to the stock-market, is flanked with the solid, tranquil inns (42) which serve a substantial 'ordinary' for the farmers on market day and may also serve the casual traveller well at other times. The broad street is so broad as to contain an old cross or monument or even substantial Guild Hall in its middle reaches without inconvenience to the thronging carts and cars of market day; such channels are capable of an island site and exquisitely it has often been used. The value of an islanded street we know from the churches in the roaring Strand as well as from the guildhalls of the leisurely farming centres. Thame, with a main street of astonishing breadth and the savour of unruffled centuries, is a typical market-town of the South. In the North I have a strong fancy for Richmond (44), crag-crested and grey, with a smell of forays and baronial campaigns, sentinel of a grim dale where it meets the fatter pastures, the half-way house between the two worlds of heather and of grass, and hinting long, comfortable pauses after bargains hardly made between the highland and the lowland men.

The spaciousness of the market-town is sometimes felt where a great expanse of road has been left marooned in full-grown towns swollen with new occupation. Those who have done the round of Shakespearean relics and memorials of Stratford-on-Avon may perhaps feel closer to the local hero's spirit if they walk down Bridge Street on a market-morning to the Clopton Bridge; here they will remember that Stratford is a peasant's place as well as a pilgrim's and that John Shakespeare's occupation of butcher and general merchant is still as important to the town as his son's more venerated craft. Oxford, too, is not all based on culture and on cars; it has never ceased to be a market-centre of the eastern Cotswolds and the Berkshire Downs. St. Giles proclaims it so. Even in London you may tumble across a similar street. Alight at the Angel, Islington, and turn north. The road to the Agricultural Hall is still, and properly, a bit of rural England. Islington was for centuries the Cockney sportsman's playground and the workshop of the old naturalists. Gerard, the herbalist, went 'simpling' in Highbury woods and the seventeenth-century fowlers pursued their game on the Islington

44 RICHMOND IN SWALEDALE, YORKSHIRE

45   BRIDGNORTH, SHROPSHIRE : A Severn Sentinel

hills. 'The citizens that come a-ducking to Islington ponds' occur in Jonson and in Davenant. Then the streams and marshes were turned into the reservoirs of the City and a market-town sprang up; the enormous breadth of road to Islington Green, with its tumble of tiled roofs and its steps up to the pavement, suggests to this day drovers and the driven, market-stalls and market crowds a-junketing.

The market-town usually offers generous satisfaction to the eye; it takes the senses. It has a history; if a chartered borough, it wrested its local freedom from the jealous powers above; it is governed by 'worshipful persons'; its atmosphere abides. It has quietude broken by a weekly clatter of livestock and chaffering salesmen. It may have fortress ruins, like Bridgnorth (45) rising in its Rhenish steepness to watch the winding Severn, or Barnard Castle, guardian of the Tees. It is good to take beef and beer in these places and wander from the Broad Street to the narrow courts and lanes, by the river and on to the Castle Crag. But, for my part, I would never care to live there; either solitude or city is one individual's preference. In small country towns everybody knows everybody and all about everybody; they are the busybodies' paradise. It is true that they know too in the village, but then there are so few people to do the knowing, the gossiping, the interfering. Let us make sentimental journeys and delight our eyes, as well as satisfying thirst and appetite, in the market-town; and so home.

The water-power of the northern hills created, during and after the Industrial Revolution of the eighteenth century, some of the most curious manufacturing towns.

I

The mills for treating cotton and wool follow the streams
up into the Pennine heather, cotton on the west, wool
on the east. The towns are often small for the simple
reason that there is no space for them to be any bigger
without climbing impossible banks. They are sandwiched
between the sheer fell-side and the water; the grey mills
are poised in a natural niche and the houses of the
workers climb away from them, up staggering hills.
Their prosperity has had its ups and downs, but they
still hang on, financially as well as physically. The population, suspended between the heathery waste and the
close-packed clutter of the town, is not quite urban, but
it is essentially homogeneous. There is virtually no
middle class. Either a man owns a mill or he works in
it. Everybody is making, or is eager to make, something;
the merchanting is done in Manchester or Leeds, where
the middle-men swarm. A rector, a doctor or two and
a few bank-managers make up the middle class of the
fell-side mill-towns. Retired folk move to softer places;
nobody is there for fun.

The great manufacturing towns of the North and
Midlands make homes for an enormous section of the
English people. The combined populations of Cheshire,
Lancashire and Yorkshire run to ten and a half millions,
of Northumberland and Durham to two and a quarter
millions, of Warwickshire and Staffordshire to another
three. The rural element in these counties is large in
acreage, but not in residents. The cities which began to
sprout at the end of the eighteenth century and have
been swelling ever since are nearly all unlovely, which is
not the same as unlikeable. They can be more easily
explained than excused. They grew when humanity had

46 OXFORD STREET, MANCHESTER

47 STEEL AND SMOKE : Night over Sheffield

48 THE METALWORKERS

49 LEEDS IN THE RAIN

50 MANCHESTER TRIES AGAIN: The new City Library

found one thing and lost another. It is the habit of epochs to let slip something of the national heritage while they add to it. The eighteenth century had lost the restless spirit which in some form is essential to a vivid and creative civilisation; but it had taste. Its self-complacence found many graceful forms of expression. The nineteenth century lost taste and it recovered the eagerness for novelty and advance just at the time when the obvious channels of new movement were mechanical and commercial. It plunged into the factory age with a greedy eye for main chances and quick results. Nobody seems to have cared much about civic appearances or civic health. There was no plan and there was not much of social conscience. So the industrial cities happened. Mills and drab rows of houses for the mill-hands were jumbled together; the centres of commerce and administration were hurriedly surrounded by squalid zones of 'industrial area.' No thought was taken for amenity or recreation. The typical manufacturing town only remembered the necessity for open spaces when the centre had all been shabbily closed. Accordingly, while most capitals have parks in the centre, because they were built with consideration and before the age of greedy hustle, the manufacturing towns have their parks on the fringe or in the suburbs. There is no dignified approach to the centre of things. Rivers were foully polluted and smoke belched from countless, uncontrolled chimney-stacks. In 1536 Manchester was described by the antiquary Leland as 'the fairest, best buildid, quickkest, and most populous towne of all Lancastreshire.' Fair and well-built were epithets which might then have been applied to all the towns that later on were to achieve simultaneously the peaks of prosperity and the depths of squalor. By 1836 the damage was begun, by 1886 it was irreparable.

By 1936? I have called the damage irreparable because the Victorian mess is too big to rebuild. The adjective is only unjustified if you can call abolition a form of repair. The Victorian débris is far too vast to abolish at one politic blow. The only practical course is to get as many people as possible out of the mess and as quickly as possible. That course, since the war, has been generally but slowly taken. People are encouraged to move out into new suburbs, which, at their dullest, are orderly and hygienic and at their best, notably in Manchester's Wythenshawe, with its park-way approaches, extremely attractive. Most of the big cities have made an attempt to atone at the edge for the crimes committed by our fore-fathers in the centre. But the trouble has been the gap between the economic rental of a new suburban house, however humble, plus cost of transport to and from work, and the ability of the present slum-dweller to pay for those things. (The problem of reconstruction is not limited to the actual slums, i.e. to houses and tenements certified as unfit for habitation, but to miles of drab little houses which are monotonous and depressing but are just habitable enough to pass an elementary test of hygiene.) The shifting of population involves many problems. It has been discovered in Middlesbrough that the standard of health declined when the occupants of slums were moved to new and infinitely healthier quarters, because the increased expenditure on rental meant decreased expenditure on food. Heavy subsidies have been applied to housing since the war; even so

51   IRON: Bilston

52 HEAVY INDUSTRY: Blast Furnaces for Steel

we cannot equip the poorest town-dwellers with decent homes without causing further economic distress. The Victorian mess abides. By our toleration of ribbon-development along main roads we are ourselves preparing the mess of to-day and of to-morrow.

It would be absurd to think of the inhabitants of any specimen Coketown as universally depressed by their surroundings; indeed, their contentment is the despair of the reformers. As far as unhappiness is concerned, it is doubtful whether the mill-workers, housed in Mean Street, are more concerned with their own miseries than are the prosperous brain-workers and cultured leisurely folk of the capital who fuss with psychology and brood over their own grievances. Graceful and beautiful birds have no aesthetic sense; swallows, with the whole of pastoral England at their disposal, will nest in the dirtiest manufacturing village, so their food be there; sea-gulls, with all our foreshores for a dining-room, come inland to a reeking dump of garbage. Men and women are able to ignore their surroundings to a comparable extent; they can accept without questioning a vile social legacy, so the food be there, and sometimes when it is not. History would be very different if they were not thus patiently adaptable.

Many people can get fond of their machines, hard masters though they be, and many also can endure without distress drudgery which seems insupportable to others: and always mankind discovers ways of escape from the monotony and fatigue of factory labour; the first victims of the Industrial Revolution drugged themselves with cheap gin. But the recourse to alcohol for purposes of 'a blind' has continually and rapidly de-

K

creased. Convictions for drunkenness fell from 200,550 in 1905 to 36,285 in 1933, a sensational decline. This is partly due to the increased cost and decreased strength of liquor, but partly to an increase of common sense and self-respect. The wild drinking of inflammable spirit, which is still an escape of the Scottish slum-dweller, is very rare in England where the popular absorption of a fairly mild ale enriches brewer and Treasury without much damage and with considerable pleasure to the recipient. There might be even less drunkenness than there still is if licensed hours were extended; in that case there would be less tendency to 'rush drinking' in the last few minutes before closing.

A new oblivion has been offered by the films which for a few coppers will offer transport, in comfortable surroundings, from Coketown to an Alsatia of ravishing blondes whose chastity is grievously menaced through eighty minutes of thrilling temptation but is finally offered intact to a miraculously handsome gentleman with a super-super-motor-car. The films have naturally driven the old melodramas out of the field; these had a long life in the mill-town circuits, but they could offer no effective competition to the cheap luxuries of the new Palasseum whose lights do at least irradiate Mean Street and break the drab monotony of dingy lace curtains in the 'two-up and two-down' houses and of slatternly shops which sadly need a coat of paint. Then there is betting, which no amount of legislation will ever suppress; afternoon betting is on horses with slips of paper and small coin furtively handed to the book-maker's tout or passed across the counter in a small shop whose owner takes a chance; evening betting takes place 'at the dogs.'

53   CHEMICALS :   Widnes

54, 55 THE POTTERIES

56, 57   THE BLACK COUNTRY

58   A DERBYSHIRE PIT-HEAD

During the last ten years the racing of greyhounds in pursuit of a mechanical hare has achieved and retained great popularity (121). The prices of entry are much smaller than at horse-race meetings and the time, after work in the evening, is far more suitable to proletarian needs; also the races follow each other in more rapid succession and quite small sums can be staked. The social menace of this form of gambling has been much cried up by the puritanically minded, who are strangely oblivious of the fact that the Stock Exchange, which is rarely, if ever, attacked, is quite as much of a casino. If stock-brokers had to exist on genuine investment and not on the dipping in and out of those who are merely 'punting,' half of them would be out of work. Smuggled tickets for big sweepstakes also bring a few thrills and a myriad disappointments to Coketown. But occasionally a little combine of mill-hands will find themselves with twenty or thirty thousand pounds. It is the modern equivalent of the fabled treasures of romance, a kind of Fairy Gold. Those who are so concerned about the gambling of the working-class also conjure up pictures, sometimes truthful, of the man who has ruined his home; they never allude to the man who has had a lucky win and has given his family a treat. Yet that does happen.

The English town-worker is a constant devotee of sport. As a small boy he played cricket and football anywhere and everywhere (113), in empty streets and on waste patches. Later he did his best to get into a team which had a pitch in a public park or on one of the grounds with which the National Playing Fields Association is endeavouring to sweeten the monotony of the built-up areas. He is an eager spectator of cricket and

football on county and town grounds (117, 118). Miners
are especially fond of racing dogs and racing pigeons are
another popular possession. On the outskirts of every
large town where there is pond, river or canal, coarse
fishing is patiently practised by large numbers of men
and boys, who will sit for hours in any weather in the
hope of some diminutive catch. It is preferable, no
doubt, to an overcrowded home with the children frac-
tious and the over-worked wife in a nagging mood.
From time to time great angling competitions are held,
at which hundreds of entrants, each with an allotted
space of river bank, eagerly count their victims by the
ounces. It is scarcely exciting to the onlooker, but it
gives infinite pleasure to the practitioner. The younger
people have lately taken to wandering afield (26); but
the 'hikers' are more often from the office than from the
factory. A hard week in the mill or the workshop inclines
to less strenuous week-ends; the motor-bicycle, with
side-car where it can be afforded, gives the Coketown
family a new liberty of the countryside, and the push-
bicycle has found renewed favour among the actively
disposed. Cycling clubs swarm out of the towns on
Saturday and Sunday. Yes, Coketown does, in a multi-
tude of ways, go about, dream dreams and forget. But
that is no reason for accepting the place with equanimity.
A home should be a place where people are content to
stay, not a base for frantic efforts at escape.

59 CEMENT : Greenhithe

60 THE SUPERIOR SUBURB: A Surrey Scene

CHAPTER VI

THE SUBURB

JUST as the heart of England may be worn on its maritime sleeve, so the heart of many English towns seems really to exist upon the suburban fringe. Allusion has already been made to the haphazard growth of the manufacturing cities whose central areas were surrounded by a confused belt of factories and workshops. Population, as it grew, had to move outward beyond this belt for decent habitation and, with quicker, cheaper transport, it recently began to move very far indeed. When the day's work is done, the centre of the town empties rapidly; a few people may linger on to visit theatres and cinemas, but after eight o'clock the centre of such a city as Manchester is strangely deserted considering the size and commercial importance of the place. The number of restaurants and cafés open is inconsiderable compared with the number in a Continental town of similar wealth and population. At week-ends it is almost a desert, a wilderness of trams clanging down empty streets. The social life has flowed outwards and the pulse of the city beats on Saturday nights in suburban homes, taverns, dance-halls and picture-palaces.

The status of the suburb in English life has been greatly heightened by the English passion for a roof of one's own. To live in flats and tenements is unusual outside of London; those who cannot have a big house insist on a small one, and the post-war housing of the workers has developed enormous suburbs, new towns even, such as

Becontree, containing countless rows of small houses instead of enormous block-dwellings on the Continental model. The Government's housing policy for 1935 inclines to replacement of slums by cheap flats, but before this the general policy was for outward instead of upward construction. The acreage and mileage swallowed up in this way has been enormous, and the speed of the process terrific, both round London and the provincial cities. Less than thirty years ago North-west London ended with the semi-rural pleasaunces of Hampstead and Highgate. Hendon and Finchley were country villages to which one bicycled, leaving London behind with its last and jovial outpost at the song-celebrated "Bull and Bush." Now nearly all Middlesex has been devoured and the process, so much assisted in pre-war times by the opening of the Tube Railway to Golder's Green, has been briskly accelerated in the last decade. Middlesex showed the greatest increase of population of any county between 1921 and 1931. During these years the people of Great Britain increased by 5·5 per cent, the people of Middlesex by 30 per cent. The exact figure of addition is 385,579.

This was partly due to migration outwards; the population of the London County administrative area continually declines, as in the interest of health it should do. It lost 87,000 people during the last census-decade. There was also migration southwards; during this period, according to Dr. H. W. Smith's valuable survey of *The Industries of Greater London*, 'the counties in the North of England have lost nearly half a million people, while the Home Counties have gained 615,000.' Their trek to the South was caused and encouraged by the

61, 62 OLD VILLAGE AND NEW SUBURB

63 SUSSEX SPREADS ITSELF

new light industries which sprang up round the edge of London; electrical power made them independent of the water, the coal-seams and the iron-deposits which conditioned the prosperity of the North. The big northern industries did not move themselves South and new industries did arise in the North and Midlands, e.g. the Billingham factory of Imperial Chemicals, the expansion of the motor-industry at Coventry and the great new ironworks at Corby in Northants. But the accretive and magnetic power of this new London has been remarkable. The new industries of Greater London, according to Dr. Smith, 'reflect directly the miscellaneous demands arising from the concentration of nine million consumers.' They depend much on the assembly of parts made elsewhere and on the service of the gigantic new market for cheap luxuries and instruments of pleasure. A similar process of decentralised factory-construction has gone on elsewhere, notably around Birmingham and at Trafford Park, near Manchester. But the London Region, which will soon be almost continuous from Southend to Maidenhead and St. Albans to Guildford, has been the greatest example of suburban dispersion.

These new factories, moving to the suburbs for cheap land and labour supply, naturally increased the suburbs yet again by necessitating thousands of homes for their workers. The arterial roads were no sooner built than ribboned with small factories and the houses of their employees, as a drive along the Great West Road or Kingston By-Pass will sufficiently prove. That the new factories are lighter, healthier, better-looking places than the old is obvious; that the new suburbs are often a tangled monotony of ill-planned villadom is equally plain (62). What strikes one as so oppressive is street after street of exact similarity in all but name; it is sometimes a marvel that the suburban house-owner, returning on a dark night from the railway station or 'bus terminus, can find his way home; any one of ten thousand little residences might be his. One may be labelled 'Elmhurst' and the next 'St. Aubyns,' but for mile after mile all are identical Brick-Box. Another melancholy feature has been the appeal to snobbery made by the people who transformed the old gardens and parklands into new villadom and turned the seigneurial Home Counties into counties of the multitudinous home. They found a farm with some plain-spoken name and they left it as Fauntleroy Park, where the house-hungry were dazzled with the offer of 'Cozy Palaces' and 'Little Baronial Halls.' Evidently they knew their market; the prospect of becoming a Little Baron sent thousands in urgent haste to the Building Societies for the mortgage needed to achieve this domestic ennoblement. Far too many of the new 'estates' are a welter of sham-Tudor villas without style or dignity of any kind. Fortunately there are exceptions, especially where public authorities, such as the L.C.C., which employed architects of distinction under the direction of Mr. Topham Forrest, have set a standard of planning and design and proved that the housing of our period need not be limited to feeble mimicries of the medieval manner.

Passing our Fauntleroy Park one is sadly struck by the absence of public buildings; there are row after row of new small houses, which consist of five or six rooms with usual offices. They are cramped places inevitably; the price dictates it; if a man wants a roof of his own (in perpetuity or until such time, perhaps not distant, when the roof falls in) and if he can only pay small deposits monthly to a final total of a few hundred pounds, he cannot expect many rooms or large. Perhaps our Little Baron has a little garage and a midget motor; if so he enjoys thereby, at the week-end, some sense of space and freedom. If not, he potters diligently in his own tiny garden. There must be growing up a huge host of suburban English who have never been in a big room on domestic premises. Nor are there many public rooms available. The ordinary urban street is diversified by church or chapel, theatre or cinema, schools, warehouses and so forth. But in these mushroom suburbs of the nineteen-twenties there is scarcely any break in the monotony of small building; here and there a cinema manages to intrude itself, but theatres are virtually unknown, inns and taverns are scarce and strictly kept so by the licensing justices; an active campaign has been launched to equip the newly built areas with churches, but many miles have been covered with streets in which the necessity for places of common assemblage, serving both to relieve the eye and to comfort the body or the soul, has been seriously overlooked. How intensely domestic we are willing to be! To a foreigner this intensive segregation into a host of identical hutches must seem one of the oddest, chilliest features of the new English suburb.

This is a dismal picture of Fauntleroy Park, but it is only objectively so. It must not be concluded that the Fauntleregians are dismal, doleful folk. It is a common notion of the urban intellectual who writes books and plays that every family of season-ticket holders with an income of less than four or five hundred pounds a year is incurably miserable. In literature the people of that class mope behind lace-curtains and water the aspidistra with incessant tears; they are mean, jealous and joyless and the affair usually ends with the seduction of the daughter and the suicide of Dad. Illness, accident and sudden loss of employment and income may befall anyone; where the luck is average, the suburban English are a cheerful people with a good notion of how to enjoy themselves and a resolute will to do so. There is ubiquitous radio to preserve the quiet evening in the home from excess of quietude. There is not only the annual holiday which is a far more regular feature of English than of foreign life; there is the proud possession of a garden, however diminutive; if the Little Baron cannot swing that inexplicable but proverbial cat indoors, he can ply a spade without. There are the Saturdays and Sundays, with possibly a small car; there are the tennis-club and bowling-green; there are jaunts to the pictures and, far more impressive, there are occasional nights 'Up West.'

The English are great 'clubbers.' They love to get behind walls and barriers; nobody wants to play lawn-tennis on public courts, however cheap and excellent, if he or she can join the Fauntleroy L.T.C. with its gate and its fence and its protection of this dear privacy by exclusion of the undesirable applicant. Snobbish? Of course it is, but how dull life would be if we never turned up a nose at anything or anybody. Your Little Baron, like anybody else, can derive a deal of satisfaction from a lifted nose. If he has money enough he will join a golf club too, but that will mean not less than five

64 SLUM CLEARANCE IN LONDON

65 EALING'S LAST WORD

66 LEAFY LEISURE : A Cheltenham Façade

guineas a year and probably more. Still, it is another place with a fence; you can keep the bounders out, unless the Club is so much in need of funds that even the wrong sort must be deemed the right. There is a nice bar (men only) as well as a common-room for both sexes. Here tales are told. So, too, where there are public rooms available, flourish whist-drives, ping-pong, badminton and dancing, November comes in; the fogs and rains descend upon the dank mud flats which once were Fogey's Farm and now compose the desirable estate of Fauntleroy Park. It is not so pleasant catching the 8.10 to Liverpool Street or Waterloo. But spirits are maintained. Joy cometh in the evening.

And especially on that Saturday evening in midwinter when the Fauntleroy L.T.C. or G.C. has its annual dinner in the West End. One of the marbled chambers (private, of course) is reserved in one of the eating-palaces best known for such junketing. It is undoubtedly a brilliant night. There is much womanly eyeing of the other woman's dress. But fellowship prevails. Ladies who 'never take anything' experiment with cocktails and wine to follow. There is a great spread, ample in all its parts from those varied hors d'œuvres, which never vary, to the *Bombe Splendide*, which never melts from the menu. Great joviality assists digestion of the banquet; the speeches of chairman and secretary, with their diligent jocosities, are duly applauded and pleasantly mitigated by the appearance of hired entertainers on the dais with the piano. A soprano announces that spring is coming and nobody is really sorry when she herself is going. But 'the comedian' is another matter. He is 'a scream' and is vigorously asked for more. At eleven the party begins to scatter. The young become sparkish and there is great fun going home, six adults to a Baby Austin. It knocks the purse pretty hard, by the standards of the Park, but it is only once a year, well worth it, and 'a good time was had by all.' There may be five thousand suicides a year in Great Britain, but they do not largely occur, as our lugubrious Chelsea authors would suggest, amid the residents of Fauntleroy Park.

67, 68 FIRESIDE AND FUNCTIONAL

69 OFF TO THE SEA

CHAPTER VII

THE WEEK-END

ACCORDING to the *Oxford English Dictionary* the word 'week-end' appeared in our language in 1878; the 'week-end ticket' followed nine years later. This English institution will be shortly due for a Golden Jubilee; this will doubtless be celebrated in kind by at least a devout few who will terminate their week of labour on Thursday and begin again on the next Wednesday. Some people's week-ends are already so elastic as to horrify the foreigner. When staying in Prague I discovered that a Czechoslovak friend of mine regarded himself as a giddy and dissolute fellow if he closed his office at five on Saturday afternoon and took a train to the hills. When I told him that many English business men would sign their last letter at five o'clock on Friday and not be back till Monday, he was amazed. With natural politeness I did not suggest that these apparent idlers probably got through as much work in a week as he did and with less fuss. Industry is not to be judged by the clock and the calendar and the happy English employment of Saturday is, after all, dependent on the ability to make a living in five or five and a half days instead of six.

The rise of the week-end depended on the decline of Sunday observance. It was not worth while to pack and depart if, during the major part of the week-end, all things were barred to the traveller save church doors. One could do one's churchgoing just as well at home. The English Sunday has been a matter of dispute for

M

hundreds of years and still is, as the wireless programmes confess. James I, when he issued his *Book of Sports* in 1618, took the sensible line of encouraging all such exercise and entertainment as did not interfere with religious offices.

'And as for our good people's lawful Recreation, Our pleasure likewise is, That, after the end of Divine Service, Our good people be not disturbed, letted, or discouraged from any lawfull recreation, vaulting, or any other such harm lesse Recreation, nor from having of May Games, Whitson Ales and Morris-dances, and the setting up of Maypoles, and other sports therewith used so as the same be had in due and convenient time, without impediment or neglect of Divine Service; and that women shall have leave to carry rushes to the Church for the decoring of it, according to their old custome. But withal we doe here account still as prohibited all unlawfull games to bee used upon Sundays onely, as Beare and Bull-baitings, Interludes, and at all times, in the meaner sort of people, by Law prohibited, Bowling.'

The angry Puritans hit back, when their time came, and not only prohibited Sunday recreations but forbade, by the act of 1650, the use of boats, coaches and sedan-chairs. By an act of 1657 the Justices of the Peace were actually entitled to invade private houses in quest of Sabbath-breakers, among whom were included any so wicked as to play musical instruments. The Restoration brought its natural reaction, but Pepys, who was now enabled to hire a boat on Sunday, adds 'God forgive me' to the information that he had been stringing a lute on the seventh day. The ordering of Sunday duties and Sunday pleasures has varied greatly since then according to the balance of power in religious politics. Victorian Evangelicals and Nonconformists reintroduced a strict

70 SUNDAY ON THE ROAD

71 NEWCASTLE : The Sunday Morning Quayside Market

discipline, from which there has been a steady decline in the South of England with the northern cities remaining more austere. That the bleakness of Sunday in a northern town is not a tyrannical imposition of the 'kill-joys' but rests on popular sentiment was proved by the recent plebiscites held on the desirability of Sunday cinemas. Generally speaking, the South voted for the opening of cinemas on Sunday evenings and the North voted against.

The great enemy of Sunday observance has been cheap and easy transport. The motor car has even crashed its way through the massive fortification of the Scottish Sabbath; if people can get to places away from home, they will demand to be served with refreshment and, if there are profits to be made, they will eventually get it. From that they will proceed to assert the right to amuse themselves, to bathe and boat, to play lawn-tennis or golf. The only English golf-clubs which forbid Sunday play are a few whose landlords make this abstinence a condition of renting the land. Their number diminishes, even in Cornwall where the Sabbatarian spirit has long remained fanatical. On most courses near towns Sunday is the busiest day of the week and often an occasion for important competitions. Even in Scotland, where to swing a club on Sunday was once deemed a hell-fire matter, there are an increasing number of courses permitting Sunday play. In the London area amateur Sunday games of all kinds are now almost universal; but professional spectacles, seeking profit, are restricted to Saturday. In the North, however, there is a far stricter regimen and young people, who want exercise but cannot afford to join golf-clubs, must take to the roads on foot or bicycle. The fact that Coketown still closes its public tennis-courts and cricket-pitches on Sunday has doubtless been a great recruiting influence for the 'hiking' movement; also it has stimulated the manufacture of bicycles and motor-bicycles and the booking of seats in public vehicles. The motor-coach is a post-Sabbatarian invention and, being born free, it has never been put in chains.

The arrival of the cheap motor-car and motor-cycle and the ubiquity of the motor-bus have, in effect, nationalised the mobile week-end, which had hitherto been the special property of the well-to-do. It is true that cheap railway tickets and the economical trips organised by the National Sunday League had already made Sunday a day of travel to some extent, but it was the poor man's motor-car, private or public, which finally overran the old notions of a tranquil and motionless leisure. This centred round a huge hot dinner at Sunday midday, which feast was naturally followed by a torpid afternoon. The solid meal, at least in summer, lost friends as rapidly as the solid sermon, and butchers have publicly complained of diminished trade because so many families take tinned food, hard-boiled eggs and jam-sandwiches on their Sunday picnic instead of sitting down to the customary sirloin or leg of lamb. It is characteristic of the obscurantist policy of the English Railways that they still seem to regard Sunday travelling, apart from cheap excursions, as a form of debauchery. The Sunday trains are fewer and slower than the week-day trains and to make a cross-country journey by rail is either impossible or an agony of extreme duration; even the crudest forms of refreshment are often unobtainable. While the Railway managers, still imagining themselves to exist in the Victorian England of the stay-at-home Sabbath, were maintaining diminished and sluggish services the motor-bus companies were doubling their number of vehicles on the road and prudently studying the needs of the new army of Sunday travellers.

For generations school-children have been compelled to write essays on 'The influence of climate on national character.' Are they now invited to expound the influence of petrol on national habit? It would be a wise teacher who encouraged them to do so, for there is no doubt that cheap, easy and all-pervasive travel by motor has enormously altered ways of living. A journey along the main road from the East Coast to London on a Sunday evening in summer is a tedious business, owing to the density of traffic, but instructive. Myriads of East Enders, packed seven or eight in an antiquated car which has been bought for a few pounds and seems almost to be held together by string and straps, are jogging home from a day at Clacton or Southend. The pace is slow, not merely because of the numbers travelling, but because the cars are so decrepit and so heavily charged with conglomerate uncles and aunts, children bunched liked bananas, bags, baskets, coats and toys that acceleration is impossible. Thirty years ago these people never left the town, except perhaps for one week in the year. Saturday night was spent in the gin-palace and Sunday morning was spent in sleeping it off. The new democratic week-end, even if it be mainly devoted to covering decent sand with orange-peel and cigarette cartons or to tearing up bluebells by the roots, is certainly the more hygienic.

The more prosperous week-enders of to-day, if they

lack country cottages of their own, frequent country clubs, usually country houses, too large to be easily let and now transformed into centres of recreation. The gardens are equipped with new tennis-courts and the inevitable swimming-pool. Possibly there is a private golf-course; certainly there are facilities for dancing. A squash-racket court may be added. A little below this in the social scale is the Road House (73), a species of sportive hotel which grew up along the new motoring roads and caters especially for the bright young person in the gaudy little car. Here too are swimming and various games; probably a couple can dine and dance there, with a few drinks, for a good deal less than a pound inclusive. Road Houses are not residential as a rule; their favourite site is about twenty minutes' run from a big town. They sprang up because the country hotel-keepers were too sleepy to realise the needs of the new motoring public and so missed their chances or because 'by-pass roads' ran through country where there were no inns at all. Their gaiety runs to garishness; in the baser type of Road House one meets the new paganism in its flashiest form. One of these institutions, advertising its pleasures, recently announced the presence of 'Super-Super-Barmaids.' It is a stirring phrase and perhaps it sums the matter up.

But they cater always for the swimmer and that is to their credit. The hot, dry summers of 1933 and 1934 confirmed a previous tendency to find pleasure in and around water. The swimming-pool appeared everywhere, and even small villages began to dam up a stream and arrange for what is incurably and ubiquitously called a Lido. One of the strangest of these in my experience

72, 73 OLD INN AND NEW ROADHOUSE

74 ' THE DOWNS SO FREE '' : A Bank-holiday Bird's-eye

was cut in a field in the bleak Derbyshire uplands. A go-ahead farmer had realised that there was more money in giving people fun than in giving them food; he actually installed a boiler to take the chill off the mountain water and soon collected patrons from the villages and small towns in the neighbourhood. Our ancestors valued dipping in cold water for medicinal reasons. It is related of a certain archdeacon of the seventeenth century that 'when he was a student in Oxford, eating too much fat Venison, he found himself extremely ill and, fearing a Surfeit, he went into the Water and swam up and down for the space of nearly two hours and came forth very well and continued so.' We have other notions about the merits of bathing in a state of 'surfeit' and are drastically warned against a plunge directly after eating. Equally we reject the seventeenth-century notion that cold water is good for a chill because 'it doth shutt up the pores of the body.' But we share Bacon's view that a good garden should have a bathing-pool, even if we cannot rise to the advice of that ever prodigal genius. His bathing-pool 'may admit much curiosity and beauty . . . as that the bottom be finely paved and with images; the sides likewise; and withal embellished with coloured glass and such things of lustre; encompassed also with fine rails of low statuas.' Our road-side Lidos, crowded haunt of the summer week-ender, are not designed with such Renaissance luxury; we leave it to the fountain-loving Swedes, whose chief sculptor, Carl Milles, has a genius for aquatic decoration, to mix the arts with the exercise. But our less ornate tanks, with the chairs and terraces for the sun-bathers, effectively cater for pleasure and health.

The youngsters of the last generation went to the Public Swimming-Bath, first class sixpence, second class fourpence, an indoor establishment with segregation of the sexes, except perhaps on one night of the week when it was conceded by authority that men and women might see each other in the water without perdition. Why cold water should be deemed an aphrodisiac I have never discovered; why Wednesday's virtue should have been Thursday's sin was another mystery. (Morality so often leads to mysterious conclusions.) The old roofed-in baths remain and are serviceable in the winter, but the tendency now is to create great open-air baths and the new suburbs are frequently supplied with large and well-equipped pools where one may bathe in water and air for sixpence and have a light meal at a very small cost. At week-ends, if the weather be encouraging, they are packed and people will wait in queues under a blaze of sun for the pleasure of cooling off in the water, which is, very properly, disinfected and kept in constant movement through the bath. The Victorian lady, who had to be swathed, skirted and stockinged before entering public water, would have stood aghast at the comparative nudism of the modern bi-sexual 'Lido.' That anybody is morally the worse for a swim and lounge in these new conditions remains to be proved; that many people are physically better for it is indisputable. In a swimming-pool we recreate in the original sense of that word; a dip in the dog-days can blessedly persuade us that a jaded body has been fashioned new for living.

For those who want a simple, cheap and strenuous week-end there are rucksack, stick and shoe-leather (76).

75   A LIVERPOOL LIDO : Wallasey

76 YOUTH HOSTEL

77 ALMA MATER

'Hiking' is an American word for long-distance travel without luggage or money in the purse; it has been misapplied to the English week-end walkers, but many of them seem to like the term and employ it. This rediscovery of walking as a pleasure has been recently assisted by the provision of Youth Hostels. The stress laid on Youth is more picturesque than preventive. I had often wondered what would happen to a man of eighty who asked for a night's lodging at a Youth Hostel. I learn that he would be gladly admitted if he were a member, as well he might be since the Youth Hostel Association has several members over ninety. The Y.H.A. was formed in 1930 and by the beginning of 1935 it had 40,000 members and 230 hostels. Its members grew by 10,000 during 1934, the majority being under twenty-five. On payment of a small subscription (half a crown a year for those under twenty-five and five shillings for those over it) the members can sleep the night for one shilling at any of the hostels. That is to say, they get a bed, blankets and facilities for cooking. They can bring their own food and pay for what they get, if meals are provided. There are some light conditions of discipline. The hostels are either old mansions and farms transformed to this new service of the rambler or buildings designed specially for the purpose. In the former category the Y.H.A. now possesses such seigneurial beauties as Derwent Hall and Hartington Hall in Derbyshire and also exquisite old houses amid the medievalism of Canterbury and Ludlow. Areas especially popular with walkers, such as the Lake District, are well equipped with hostels and Y.H.A. trampers may spend a night in the dark heart of the highest English

mountains, namely at Black Sail Hut at the head of En-
nerdale. While the pedestrian week-ender is greatly in-
debted to the Y.H.A., his freedom and happiness are
also much derived from the excellent work done in the
past by the Commons, Open Spaces and Footpaths
Preservation Society, vigilantly guarding 1,600,000 acres
of common land and 300,000 footpaths, the Council
for the Preservation of Rural England and the National
Trust, which acquires by gift or purchase lands and
buildings of rare beauty or historic interest for purposes of free access and general enjoyment.

78 TRENT BRIDGE : A Test Match Saturday

79　AN ANCIENT FOUNDATION IN A MODERN SETTING : The Bluecoat School at Horsham

CHAPTER VIII

THE YOUNG IDEA

THE English school is a common and conspicuous sight. There, primary and proletarian, it stands amid the city streets, the asphalt yard about its dull red brick, a play-time paradise of din; there, secondary and select, it hides among the trees of the suburb and the seaside town, projecting the inevitable playing-field beneath the shade of elms. On this sward, according to a nine-teenth-century notion but little dwindled in the twentieth, the steel of character is forged and the battle of life is won. Thomas Gray saw only buxom health and lively cheer upon the Eton meadows; it remained for Arnold of Rugby and Bowen of Harrow to make the playing-field the ally of the pulpit, to visualise cricket-captains courageous as the ideal product of an English education and to raise bat and ball as ethical instruments to the lofty pinnacles of the curriculum. If young women, now promoted to play 'Test Matches' with Australia, are physically inadequate to football, they can, with the hockey-stick, proceed

> 'To chase the rolling circle's speed
> Or urge the flying ball.'

(What dreadful stuff Gray could be moved to write by the spectacle of his old school!) So girls can also enjoy the supposedly purifying effects of violent exercise. Boys must have 'goals' to beleaguer, that they may not girls pursue in fancy or in fact. Miss E. Arnot Robinson, in an essay called "The Potting-Shed of the English

Rose" in a composite volume on *The Old School*, begins,

' "Run about girls, like boys, and then you won't think of them." That was Sherborne.'

Cricket, she adds, was compulsory at Sherborne, and she makes "Run, girls, run" the refrain of her piece. She adds that no misfortune could make her so unhappy as she was at school. Her record does not fit in with Gray's picture of children playing ball, so blissfully ignorant of Sin, Poverty, Death and all the adult misery to follow. Probably such infelicity is not a general experience. But, as you wander past the ubiquitous playing-fields, you will see them at it. "Run, girls, run! Come on, School!" So the carnal vice is exorcised—or thought to be—and some, not apt with their legs, grow faint in this obligatory quest of healthy minds in healthy bodies.

The governing of the English child has itself been continually governed by radically diverse preconceptions about human nature. On the one hand it has been held that the child is a limb of Satan abounding in original sin, only redeemable by the rod; on the other it has been as strongly opined that heaven lies about us in our infancy, that we are natural saints corrupted by the passing years and the fleshly prison, whose shades grow darker with the flight of time. The former view has been far the more popular and it brutally dominated English education for many centuries, during which the child was 'in stripes' more often than St. Paul or the Christian martyrs. Children were to have the devil expelled by force, whereas now we purge by persuasion that new Beelzebub, the complex, or kill it by kindness. Thackeray spoke of 'torture' as normal to English schooling and

80, 81 SCHOOL CRICKET: Sedbergh and Camden Town

82　THE PLAYING FIELDS OF ETON

83　THE COALFIELDS OF DURHAM

84 PRIMARY EDUCATION

85 LINING UP FOR THE SHOW

87 HARROW

86 ETON

the Christ's Hospital, whither Lamb, Coleridge and Leigh Hunt came to suffer, had little in its discipline which we can imagine Christ approving. These hard schools—for Westminster and Eton with their Busby and their Keate were no gentler—managed to be nurses of genius none the less. The scholastic triumphs did somehow emerge from all the moral terrorism.

Think, too, of the schools in Dickens, not merely of Dotheboys, a particular scandal, remote upon the York-shire moors, but of Mr. Creakle's academy at Salem House, in which there is no suggestion of exceptional squalor or cruelty. It was not for the unfortunates of the world, since J. Steerforth attended, along with David Copperfield. It was just what passed for education in early Victorian England. Of course the savagery was reciprocal. You cannot treat boys as limbs of Satan without promoting Satanic reactions. What they suffered at the hands of Mr. Creakle they returned upon the inoffensive head and shoulders of Mr. Mell. As they were treated so they behaved, and the persecuted usher was quite as pitiful a product of the system as the bullied child. Somehow or other the pupils learned things in these places and came out to do well in the world. But, when people scoff at progress, the history of schooling in this country affords one of the best arguments with which to meet them. Squalor and incompetence there still may be, but a man like Creakle would be in the police-court in a week.

The Romantic Movement restored the notion of the little angel, implicit in Wordsworth's picture of a pigmy darling, and the Victorian 'Doctor,' though he certainly did not abandon the cane as the magic wand of wisdom and of virtue, changed Thwackum's happy tune. He was prone to whimper piously over the sad necessity of thus dislodging Satan instead of frankly enjoying the process. The famous snivel of 'This hurts me more than it does you' began to be heard in the headmaster's study and to inform scholastic theory. The eighteenth-century flagellants would have spurned such cant; they were doing a pleasurable duty and conforming, like devout men, to Solomon's instruction. Were they to be ashamed of the birch with its Biblical sanction? Social approval was all on Solomon's side and even the victims would announce in after life that hard knocks had made them what they were, assuming thereby a status of moral paragon. Nowadays there are still practitioners of the good old rules and simple plans, but the moral regimen has been mitigated while the 'grand old fortifying curriculum' has been expanded to admit other subjects than much Latin and more Greek.

'Education' properly means leading not driving, and children are now encouraged to express themselves instead of blindly to obey; the prospectus of a thoroughly modern school is full of liberal theory about self-development, which would have seemed mere lunacy to an eighteenth-century schoolmaster. Mr. Max Beerbohm once observed that, if it was the duty of the English public school to knock the nonsense out of boys, it was equally the duty of Oxford and Cambridge to put it back. This wasteful process of cancellation is not as necessary as it was; quite a number of up-to-date children are free to be as nonsensical as they please, long before they have reached the mental enfranchisement of undergraduate status. To previous generations the break between school and University was enormous; to 'go up' to Oxford and

88　STATELINESS AND SCHOLARSHIP: Stowe School

89　ETON STEEPLECHASE: Toppers and Croppers

90 CLIFTON DRILLS

91 OXFORD SAUNTERS

Cambridge was to enter on a larger liberty, to sniff the air of a new, unregimented world, and to eat the forbidden fruit of unselected books, uncensored opinions. But to those coming from the new 'free school,' where children come, go, and learn as they please, that which was once a glorious liberty may seem to be a silly bondage. They will be meeting an imposed discipline for the first time in their lives.

But, whether the modern parent favours the old regimen or the new anarchy, he (or she) is determined to get the children out of the home, if the fees of a boarding-school can possibly be met. It is on this point that we differ most from foreign nations and from such near neighbours as the Scots, who are still not ashamed to make use of their excellent day-schools. England has its great day-schools, very often ancient and well-endowed foundations, which have maintained a far higher standard of teaching and of scholarship than many of the expensive boarding-schools to which the young are despatched in thousands. But the laziness of parents who cannot be bothered with children about the home and the snobbishness of others who think that the local day-school lacks 'tone' strongly support the English habit of expelling the young for thirty-eight weeks in the year. It has always seemed to me extraordinary that middle-class parents will save and scrape in order to pay one hundred and fifty or two hundred pounds a year, and even more, in order to procure an education which can be supplied, usually in far better quality, at the end of a 'bus-ride for forty or fifty pounds or even less. 'The old school tie' acquired at such cost may have more social value and the possibility of earning distinction as an athlete may be greater; but the teaching at the day-schools and grammar-schools is usually better, as may be discovered by studying the lists of scholarships won at the Universities. These are less and less monopolised by the expensive and fashionable boarding-schools. For parents with limited incomes it would surely be a far better investment to send a boy or a girl to a day-school and devote the money thus saved to enabling a University career instead of lavishing all the education funds on membership of a boarding-school and then denying the pleasures and opportunities which the University can offer.

If the English child does not enjoy school nowadays at least it can be said that he or she never had a greater chance to do so. The rigour of discipline is less and the pressure of compulsory athleticism, which used to afflict the slow and clumsy child, though it still has strongholds, has been reduced. Perhaps 'Run, girls, run' is turning into 'Trot, girls, trot' and the missing of a catch at cricket is no longer an infamy. The young men and women of to-day who take up teaching seem to me altogether more intelligent than their predecessors at the desk and dais; many of the elderly assistant-masters of my boyhood's time were so obviously failures who could just earn the poor pittance they received by in-efficiently teaching what they had in youth inadequately learned; they were mental mechanics, following the routine, never innovating, never freshening, a sad com-pany. The young masters of to-day, of whom I have met many devoting a fortnight, at the end of the long, exact-ing summer-term, to attending Summer Schools at Oxford on educational method, are a new class alto-gether; they really seem to care; they have broadened the whole basis of the dominie's work and they are permitted to range over a far broader and more liberal curriculum than was administered thirty years ago.

When I was at school, I learned small French and no German, no science whatever, and not much English history or literature; from fifteen onwards virtually the whole of my time was devoted to Latin and Greek. This intense specialisation did the requisite trick and gained me a University scholarship, but it was a grotesque training for life in the twentieth century, and I am happy to believe that nothing so absurd continues. It was not so bad in my own case, because I liked the classics, but for others of different taste and capacity it was intellectual mutilation. Moreover I had the luck to come under one or two masters who could, by their sympathy and imagnation, rise above the drab ritual of factual instruction, make ancient poetry, even to a boy, a source of pleasure and excitement, and transmute dead languages to living things. My gratitude to these men is intense and it is good to believe that their number increases.

The move to a University is not, as I have said, so great a liberation as it used to be, since, while the regulation of school-life grows looser, the Undergraduate's freedom to spend time and money (or rather credit) as he will has been somewhat curtailed. In any case three or four years at a University seem to me the best investment that a parent can make for son and daughter. Not so long ago one might have questioned so general a statement with reference to women. Up to the time of the war the women's colleges at Oxford and Cambridge were too serious and strenuous for all but the uncommonly gifted or the extremely industrious. Women were so much on their mettle in those years of disputed equality that many of them worked too hard in order to

o

justify their claim to those opportunities which the young men were taking so casually, almost as a right. The woman undergraduates were segregated and dedicated, the novice-nuns of culture. The University curricula of the Honours Schools were extensions of what a clever boy would have learned at his school and the women, who had often begun with a rather different training, were under handicap. They toiled indefatigably and sometimes grew faint in the process. But now women can and do lead more normal lives in the older Universities; they are no longer on the defence, no longer strictly secluded, no longer so merciless with themselves. They have been known to idle and enjoy themselves; they have become as their brothers and many, I imagine, are the better for sharing the masculine refusal to be too much fussed by the tasks of to-day and the exams of to-morrow.

The great majority of students, of course, are not at Oxford and Cambridge. Of 38,635 undergraduates attending English Universities in 1933–4, less than a quarter were members of the two older foundations. London University is far bigger than Oxford and Cambridge put together. But the nine modern Universities are handicapped by the position held in public life and esteem by the two ancients. These tend to draw off the exceptional students with their scholarships and exhibitions. Thus the most promising boys at a big City grammar-school are more likely to go up to Oxford and Cambridge than to proceed to their local University. Despite the brilliant academic staff and high standards at the latter, honours won at the former are more valuable afterwards and life there is more pleasant.

Nearly all Oxford and Cambridge men and a pre-

92   LIGHT AND AIR : Physical Culture at a County School

93   OXFORD BICYCLES, MAGDALEN BRIDGE

95 "TAX NOT THE ROYAL SAINT WITH VAIN EXPENSE": King's College Chapel, Cambridge

ponderant number of women 'live in College' at some time of this undergraduate career; I have stated a case for the day-boy and day-girl at school, but there is every reason for living on the premises at a University or at least in some collegiate hostel. The idle, it is true, have greater temptation to careless fleeting of the time when company is close, congenial and convivial; but the reasonable student, engaged on a University course, can learn at least as much by working things out with his or her fellows as will be derived from the many lectures and little tuition which Universities provide. To talk all night about heaven and earth and all that in them is constitutes a major and a valuable element of University life, and the man or woman in college will find this far easier than will those dispersed in lodgings. The solid reading can and should be done in vacation rather than in term. Attendance at lectures is imposed as a test of diligence and the lecturing system is historic; that is all there is to be said for it, except in some rare cases where the Lecturer happens to be a magnetic personality. But most lecturing is a routine dictation of that which can be more rapidly derived from books. The lecturing system is really based on the medieval notion that printing is a strange and novel craft and books scarce or unobtainable. It is a waste of time for both teachers and taught; far the most useful instruction is given in tutorial hours when a don meets a small group of students to hear their essays, comment thereon and generally discuss the points at issue.

The particular pleasures of Oxford and Cambridge owe little to the climate, which is depressing in both places, but much to residence in a town where books and ideas, knowledge and opinion are regarded as the essence of life. Here the thoughtful person is not an exile, as in most English towns, but a native. His own place may possess only a single book-shop; here are three or four within so many hundred yards—and good ones, richly stored. All games and sports are available and none compulsory. Young women may keep up the running recommended at school for their physical and moral salvation; but they can walk, if they choose to risk perdition. The pleasures of the river are overrated. At both Oxford and Cambridge the summer term comes so early that the number of days congenial to basking and bathing is not great as a rule. But the presence of rivers, offering the penalty of winter's mists and rheums, pays its ocular dividend in May and June. Both cities are as rich in noble lawns as in noble building (94, 95) and both Universities, maintaining Chairs on the most recondite subjects, decline to have Professors of Architecture. Here are two towns which contain the loveliest heritage of a craft whose social and aesthetic importance is paramount. But both, rejoicing in architecture's treasures, deny it academic status. Both, it may be added, have Professors of Arabic. English education is full of queer omissions. How many who attend Oxford or Cambridge ever learn anything about the history or beauty of the University or even of their own college? Only those who choose to find out for themselves, a mere handful. I suggest that, at the end of the first year, every undergraduate should be given some slight examination on these things. The knowledge would be worth far more than much which is absorbed. The young eye, directed to a beauty which it otherwise neglects, may discover new enjoyments and feed the young idea.

96   " SCHOOLS "   AT   OXFORD

97 DEMOCRACY (English Brand)

CHAPTER IX

MATTERS OF OPINION

To indict a whole nation is, as Burke reminded us, impossible; even to generalise in milder ways about the mind of a country is dangerous; but certain things may be said of the English habit of thought. Our island site has enabled us to absorb Continental notions, but they have suffered a slight and often beneficent sea-change in the process of arrival. The distance, though not great, has lent mollification to the views. Our language is itself a compound of the various deposits left by the invaders and England has usually turned out to be a good place for mixing. Our blend of Latin and of Saxon has made a noble tongue, as the English Bible and the English poets proclaim. It was lucky for us that the Bible happened to be translated just when our English language was at the top of its form. But the reason for that show of form was, once more, the adaptability of England and its excellent fertility as a mating-ground. The richness of our Tudor literature was largely due to the happy marriage of the European renaissance with our native thought and speech of the people. The classicism, diffused from abroad, ran but rarely to pedantical conclusions at home. Lyly could be too affected, Jonson, on occasion, too laboured. But for the most part the Renaissance was well digested with the gastric juice of English common sense. Shakespeare, as he touched his Italian tales with English beauty, is the perfect example of that intellectual hospitality which welcomed

P

the foreign beauty on equal terms and made no slavish surrender. Our lyric poetry of that period was a joint product of the Italian city and the English field; the two strains of blood commingled to produce a strain of rare loveliness in mood and melody.

The English mind, in the same way, has managed as a rule to accept foreign doctrine without becoming doctrinaire. It has been a Free Trader in ideas, but the change of climate has usually softened the edges of an imported philosophy. Religious contention provokes the most savage types of exacerbation and the sixteenth and seventeenth centuries witnessed the abominations of persecution on both sides of the Reformation's battle-field. But the result was the Church of England, which, offering High and Low roads with the same exquisite liturgy to the heavenly pilgrim, has proved a typically receptive institution. A worshipper can be very nearly a Roman Catholic or very nearly a Nonconformist (some would add very nearly an atheist) and remain within the National Church. In faith, as in letters, the English power of absorption has proved conveniently sound. The disadvantage, of course, of so easily acceptable a faith is lack of fervour. There have been times when the Church of England seemed to be doing nothing in particular and not even doing that very well. But out of its complacence the Church has repeatedly been stirred by new campaigners; fanaticism is not in the natural blood, but amid the English clouds and rains there often flourishes a misty genius which apprehends by intuition. Saints and visionaries have arisen to be the scourge of that lethargy which is the natural vice correlative to the English virtue of a tolerant mind.

As a nation we have preferred impulse to logic. A clear instance of that is to be seen in the history of English Socialism. Karl Marx came to England for safety, and amid the tranquillities of the British Museum he composed a book which few have read and many talk about, a book whose economic reasoning, as dull as drastic, was to shatter an Empire, but has scarcely touched, as yet, the nation in whose sanctuary it was composed. Karl Marx lies buried in Highgate cemetery, jostled in his narrow grave by the prouder tombs of the London merchants and the English middle-class. A Russian script and a few red flowers adorn it as a rule. What a queer stranger it is! The father of contemporary Communism rests in a country which let him alone in life and lets him lie in death, still unregarded, on the hill-side made far more famous by Sir Richard Whittington, that perfect type of the bourgeois struggling to prosperity. Marx formulated a scientific Socialism, and in politics the English are rarely, if ever, scientific. We drive at practice, premeditate little and derive such doctrine as we own from the dictates of a simple conscience, which proclaims the equal rights of man, or from an aristocratic tradition, which denies them. One party, dwindled now, accepts the historical fact of the poor man at rich castle's gate; it does not argue the case, but asserts a precedent. The other also does not argue; it announces that the rank is but the guinea-stamp and that the common labourer is Nature's aristocrat.

> 'When Adam delved and Eve span
> Who was then the gentleman?'

English radical theory has never wholly changed that medieval tune.

It is interesting to read the autobiographies of the older English labour leaders; nearly all acknowledge that they drew their equalitarian sentiments from Christianity. They began as Bible politicians; their Socialism, when they came to it, was emotional and intuitive, not scientific in the Marxian sense. The poetry of Burns has had a greater effect on England, especially in the North, than most people suppose, and Victorian democracy owed much to its poets who are now, for the most part, forgotten. The natural virtue of man, corrupted by poverty or squalid environment, was a constant theme of the radical lyricists of the nineteenth century. Three Scots, Robert Buchanan, David Gray and Alexander Anderson, Gerald Massey, a Buckinghamshire lad who became an errand-boy in London, and Joseph Skipsey, whose father was shot by a special constable during a strike, were much read and recited by the 'advanced' workers of Victorian England. Professor Ifor Evans in his admirable volume on *English Poetry in the Later Nineteenth Century* has included a useful chapter on the democratic songsters who succeeded the Corn-Law and Chartist rhymers. He quotes Skipsey's lyric of the miner's call to work.

> ' "Get up!" the caller calls, "Get up!"
> And in the dead of night,
> To win the bairns their bite and sup,
> I rise a weary wight.
>
> 'My flannel dudden donn'd, thrice o'er,
> My birds are kissed, and then
> I with a whistle shut the door
> I may not ope again.'

The last line has a sting in it. While Swinburne sum-

98 CHURCH OF ENGLAND

99, 100 POLITICAL LEFT AND RIGHT

moned the middle-class to a romantically rebellious state of mind, these simpler men were singing songs of freedom that worked their way into the consciousness of the manual workers.

The English Labour leaders have always tended to be emotional democrats, and as Socialists they are readier with oratory on the platform than with plans in the committee-room. All good things come from the heart, but they must go round by the head. The agnostic middle-class Fabian heads did the scheming. The natural weakness of Socialism intuitively reached has been a certain flabbiness of mind much despised by the scientific Marxian. The compensating virtue has been the absence of the fanatic's brutality. Compared with other nations, we have managed our social conflicts without much relapse into atrocity. Our flair for compromise is familiar. A Communist would say that this is because the workers are betrayed by their leaders and left irresolute to a slow attrition and an ultimate surrender. But, whichever way you care to read the history of English politics, the fact remains that we recently passed through a General Strike of nearly a week's duration without the loss of a single life, while in other countries a public meeting can hardly be called on a contentious issue without homicidal results. Our big open-air demonstrations release more violence of language than of deed. Within a few minutes' walk of my house there appears every Sunday morning a Fascist speaker in black shirt who roars his creed within five yards of an equally vehement Socialist and an orator on behalf of World Jewry. The crowd smiles and no ambulance is needed, which must seem strange to certain foreigners.

The debt of English radical opinion to Biblical sources can be further traced in the vigorous prose style of the old pamphleteers, which is rich in metaphor and cadence. To match the literature of the Chartists with the dull, cliché-ridden stuff of modern propaganda is to realise both the powers conveyed by the old self-schooling and the influence of Jacobean English on the Victorian working-class. Here is an extract from the First National Petition of 1839.

'We are bowed down under a load of taxes; which, notwithstanding, fall greatly short of the wants of our rulers; our traders are trembling on the verge of bankruptcy; our workmen are starving; capital brings no profit and labour no remuneration; the home of the artificer is desolate, and the warehouse of the pawnbroker is full.'

'Heaven has dealt graciously with our people; but the foolishness of our rulers has made the goodness of God of none effect.'

Going further back, to the Nore Mutiny of 1797, we find the delegates of the Lower Deck composing thus,

'Shall we, who amid the rage of the tempest and the war of jarring elements, undaunted climb the unsteady cordage and totter on the topmast's dreadful height, suffer ourselves to be treated worse than the dogs of London Streets? Shall we, who in the battle's sanguinary rage, confound, terrify and subdue your proudest foe, guard your coasts from invasion, your children from slaughter, and your lands from pillage—be the footballs and shuttlecocks of a set of tyrants who derive from us alone their honours, their titles and their fortunes? No, the Age of Reason has at length revolved.'

It is on the florid side, certainly. But could the far better educated sailors of to-day write anything but the jaded formulae of protest? The literature now despatched at

101, 102 QUEUES: Dole and Escape

103, 104 PROTEST AND PRACTICE : Peace Procession and Naval Gunnery

election-times is such stale, tedious, colourless stuff that
it partly explains the apathy of voters.

During the last century we may trace a steady tendency
of English opinion in the direction of Liberal–Labour
views. The country can be coaxed into voting Conservative in times of national crisis, during or after a war or
in a period of economic confusion and general appre-
hension. But the votes are thrown for security, not
reaction, and, when it comes to the point, the Conserva-
tives have rarely wished to live up to their name. Disraeli
had a far more radical mind than Gladstone and the
younger members of the Conservative party to-day
include the freshest brains in the House of Commons.
The Labour Party, especially on its Trade Union side,
has little invention or resilience of thought. It loves a
formula. The chief change in English opinion during
recent years has been the eclipse of Liberalism, so
powerful during the nineteenth century. Labour has
stolen the Radical thunder and an electoral system which
allows neither Alternative Vote nor Proportional Representation inevitably and unfairly destroys the weaker
party of the three. There seems to have been a considerable weakening of the Nonconformist vote, which used to
go solidly Liberal and preserved as Liberal strongholds
many of the country districts, notably in East Anglia and
in Devon and Cornwall. The more Radical Nonconformists have gone over to Labour, while the others have
evidently weakened both in their chapel-faith and in their
fear that Toryism means Church-rule. Religion has
increasingly drifted out of party politics, an advantage
to both. There is far more sympathy than of old between
the various Churches; with regard to such larger matters

as international peace and the League of Nations the sects are now eager to co-operate in the instruction and direction of public opinion.

The moulding of the public mind has enormously altered with the general decline in the authority of social tradition. A great deal is said about the power of the Press. But generalisation on that subject is dangerous. When the popular Press was overwhelmingly Conservative, as in 1906, the popular vote was overwhelmingly Liberal. Nor did the violent attacks on Liberalism overthrow it in the two elections of 1910. When Labour had a poorly supported daily paper it did far better at the polls than in 1931, when it had a paper with a huge circulation. 'Die-hardism' has no backing in the country comparable to the newspaper propaganda which it intermittently commands. Recent political history makes it abundantly plain that the Englishman does not vote as Fleet Street commands. Nor can attacks from Fleet Street unseat a politician who is approved by the general judgment of his party or his nation. The more, for example, that Mr. Baldwin is vilified and ridiculed in certain quarters, the stronger does his position appear to be. The advice to boycott the so-called 'Peace Ballot' of 1934—a kind of 'straw' vote on British adherence to the League of Nations and the 'collective security' system—only advertised it. The numbers voting were much larger than was generally expected.

The truth about the great popular newspapers of to-day is that they are becoming increasingly a section of the Industry of Entertainment. They are bought less for instruction than as something to look through idly. They offer, from time to time, bribes to circulation in the

THE NEW FACE OF FLEET STREET

106 DUCAL HOUSING : Blenheim Palace

107 DOCKLAND HOUSING: Deptford

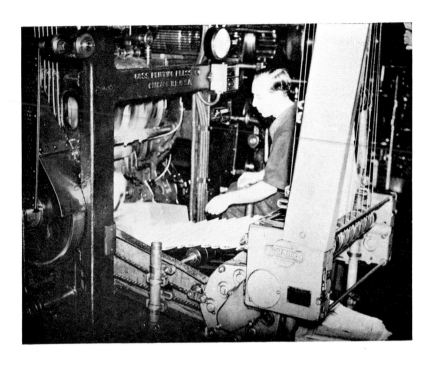

108, 109 NEWS: From Print to Purchase

way of free insurance or sets of books, which are either
free or supplied at a cost far below ordinary prices. Continually they offer distraction in the way of competitions
and puzzles. The 'feature' side of a popular paper, that
is its serial or short fiction, its picture-page, its special
articles, which hover uncertainly between the Nature
of God and the habits of murderers, as though the
editors could not decide between the rival claims of the
New Jerusalem and the Old Bailey, its special supple-
ment for children, its gossip, its cartoons, its comic
column, often brilliantly conducted, and its various
'stunts,' gain ground at the expense of the 'news and
views' which were the old and natural stock-in-trade of
journalism. Consequently there is a decreasing tendency
to take the Press seriously and a growing tendency in
return to substitute head-lines for articles and pictures
for reading-matter. Modern sub-editing appears to be
based on the notion that glancing has replaced reading,
and the newspapers which it produces become a patch-
work of bright, scrappy, amusing, or sensational items.
The public is more entertained than instructed, more
diverted than impressed.

The influence of the wireless in the formation of
public opinion is now undoubtedly very strong. In the
United States to have a good 'mike-side' manner is a
first asset to a President or to the critics of Presidents and,
though the power of broadcasting is probably less in
this country, it is none the less influential, especially
at election times. Then a speech by a party leader has
a nation-wide audience and, if he is master of an intimate,
persuasive manner, he may sway an enormous number
of votes. In America, with its commercial control of

broadcasting, anybody with funds can command an audience; it remains for his skill to retain and expand it. In England political broadcasts are strictly rationed and there are not many occasions on which controversial speeches are permitted. For that reason they are all the more important when they do enjoy the freedom of the air. The influence of wireless information and critical talks about books, plays and music has been proved to be considerable. Within the last decade an entirely new factor has thus been added to the constituents of public taste and judgment. Few would deny that it has been, on the whole, discreetly used. Wireless has also become a contributor to general education and the Broadcasts to Schools are conducted with a nice mixture of imagination and common sense. The dramatic method is employed to make chronicles more graphic and, if the young do not enjoy these half-hours of History Without Tears, it is not for want of sympathy in the speakers and technical skill in the projection of their lesson.

Any young person of to-day who really intends to store his or her mind can do so at trifling expense. Not only is there free progress up the educational ladder for the scholarship children, but, after schooling, public libraries, the classes provided by the Workers' Educational Association, with first-class tutors, and the resources of the Polytechnics are all at their disposal either free or for very small sums of money. In London ballet, opera and classical drama can be enjoyed for a few pence at the 'Old Vic' and Sadler's Wells Theatres and, as has been said, the wireless, intelligently used, provides an education in itself.

That the public mind is better informed than in

III LONDON PARADE GROUND

previous generations must, I think, be true. That it is more alert, critical and independent remains to be shown. The danger of so much free information is that it will be uncritically absorbed. There is a certain truth in the notion that the unlettered worker has a native common sense which his better-schooled successor may lose amid his larger vocabulary and his wider cognisance with theory. It can hardly be said that the nationalisation of knowledge by general education has justified itself as yet in England. But, once the path of universal schooling has been trodden, there is little use in looking backward with regrets; we must plod on and hope to create a public mind which is proof against catch-words and slogans and able to penetrate below the surface of attractive words and phrases to the essential meaning. That is the real function of public education.

CHAPTER X

RECREATION

Many people find their relief from one kind of work by application to another. Weeding a garden seems to me the most deterrent form of labour, a bore and a back-ache abominably mixed; but numbers of urban workers, who could quite well afford to hire a gardener, delight to delve and scrape on summer evenings. In the same way a man who has spent eight hours at a counter or machine will devote his winter evenings to self-imposed 'lessons.' At least that is what a schoolboy would call the classes and study-circles of the Workers' Educational Association, which attracted more than sixty thousand students in 1934. A proportion of these, when their summer holiday arrives, spend it at a Summer School in a University town. Oxford in vacation is no longer the desert which Charles Lamb so happily encountered, finding 'the groves of Magdalen' to be as good as his own property. Through July and August the halls, lawns and quadrangles are packed with tutors and taught, keenly disputatious groups from offices, factories and workshops, who bring to economic theory a wider acquaintance with hard economic fact than is common to the usual occupants.

But games are the traditional form of English recreation, and of these cricket is the traditionally English example. Football, more especially the Association game, has become international; its appeal out-distances all limitations of class and colour. The Malays, for

112 NEWCASTLE FAIR: The Arrival of the Roundabouts

113 BACK-ALLEY FOOTBALL

114 RUGGER AT RICHMOND

instance, adore it. But cricket is almost entirely limited
to English-speaking peoples. In England its history has
been a long one; according to Mr. Samuel Looker's
excellent *Anthology of Cricket* the first of our cricket poets,
a large tribe, was Joseph of Exeter, A.D. 1180, who
announced that

> 'The youths at cricks did play
> Throughout the merry day.'

Even gloomy fellows like "The Shropshire Lad" found
solace in the same sport.

> 'Every May time to the wicket,
>   Out I march with bat and pad;
> See the son of grief at cricket,
>   Trying to be glad.'

Cricket for some centuries was regarded by authority
as a Bad Thing, because it deflected young men from the
practice of archery; Kipling's opinion of 'flannelled
fools' was shared by Edward IV, in whose reign cricket-
ing was a punishable offence. It is the more curious,
therefore, that the game should have become in the
opinion of Victorian moralists the best of all Good
Things, the perfect discipline of youth. It was owing to
them that the phrase 'playing cricket' became synony-
mous with fair dealing and gentlemanly conduct. But there
is no doubt that the originators of the game as we know
it (a very different matter from the medieval 'cricks'),
the aristocratic patrons and their plebeian players of the
eighteenth century, might be described as a tough lot.
The game was then played for large money-wagers.
One match on Chelsea Common, for £5 a head, ended
with violence and broken heads. We read that in

1735 'a great match at Cricket has been made between
H.R.H. the Prince of Wales and the Earl of Middlesex
for £1,000.' The Hambledon men were ready for hard
knocks and hard drinking, their liquor, according to
Nyrem, 'ale that would flare like turpentine' and punch,
'John Bull stuff—stark—that would stand on end—
punch that would make a cat speak. Sixpence a bottle!'

Then the moralists and sentimentalists annexed the
game and confused it with a moral exercise for the young,
who were continually exhorted to 'play up and play the
game.' Some, most rashly, regarded cricket as a bond of
peace and the cement of Empire, on which view recent
Anglo-Australian disputes, so bitter as actually to harass
statesmen, are sufficient commentary. As a matter of fact,
the greatest of all Victorian cricketers, W. G. Grace, was
well known as a pretty sharp customer in his attitude to
the game, and the poet Francis Thompson actually wrote
of him as 'the long-whiskered doctor that laugheth rules
to scorn.'

But cricket, whether played, as of old, in a hot atmosphere of betting and swilling or transmuted to an ethical
exercise for the betterment of English muscles and morals,
remains at the heart of England. I have already written
of the village-green; walking through a small Derbyshire
town one summer afternoon I attempted to make some
purchases; in vain, the shops were open but unattended.
The whole population was at the end of the street,
looking at a cricket 'cup final' played on a patch of grass
wedged by the river-side. Not men only, but women and
children were there. A fig for commerce. County cricket,
largely professional, has become very slow and dull,
but it is well enough supported to continue. And a

115 THE FUN OF THE FAIR

116 SHOOTING A FILM

119 LAWN TENNIS STARS AT WIMBLEDON

Test Match against Australia sweeps all other news off
the front page of a paper. The chief events of such a game,
through wireless reports, are known across the land
almost as soon as they have happened. During the last
match of the 1934 series I was walking in some wild
northern country, but I was never at any loss for hourly
knowledge of the great event. As I passed remote
cottages I was met, almost without asking, with the news
from the Oval that Bradman and Ponsford were still in.

England is becoming a land of arenas (117, 118). The
desire to be a spectator and the means to pay for that
pleasure continually increase. Bigger and better grand-
stands appear, but the more are put up the less, it seems,
are we able to get a seat in them. Lord's Cricket Ground
must have doubled its accommodation since I first went
there, but a Test Match could fill it twice over. Wimbledon used to be a nice club tennis ground; now it is what
the sporting papers call an 'International Venue' (119) and
frantic fanciers of the game are chaffering in January for
the right to a seat in June. The Twickenham Rugby
Union Football Ground, which holds 70,000 at a pinch,
could easily gather 100,000 for an international match,
if the other 30,000 had any hope of getting places.
Wembley Stadium takes more than 100,000 for the
Association 'Cup Final' in April. More would go if
they expected room to be available. Golf can hardly
be played in front of a grand-stand, so the spectators,
whom modern transport can deliver in crowds at the
most remote places, scamper all over the courses (120) and
often defeat the efforts of an army of stewards to control
the jostling mob.

Golf was long a Scottish game, erupting occasionally

and to the general surprise on English soil. A man was hanged at Banff in 1637 for stealing golf-balls; the great Scottish clubs like the Honourable Company mixed golf and claret liberally throughout the eighteenth century; the Company's records tell of one honourable offender who was 'fined only in Six Pints.' At his own request he was 'fined in Three Pints More.' Scottish golf, a Tory sport, drank itself into frenzy singing 'Awa, Whigs, awa,' and evoked its poet, Carnegie of Pitarrow, whose *Golfiad* contains the portentous couplet

'The game is ancient, manly, and employs
In its departments women, men, and boys.'

He was famed for putting as well as for poetry and one can only hope that the former was better than the latter. But England remained aloof and ignorant. As late as 1874 the *Daily News* sent a reporter to Blackheath to investigate the mystery. He described 'Hardy Scotchmen in scarlet jackets and white breeches, preceded by a scout carrying a red flag and attended by costermongers out of work, each of whom carries an armful of implements.' The investigator concluded that none but stag-shooting Highlanders from the misty isles would thus pertinaciously plod across the wilds of Blackheath on a cold morning. But English nineteenth-century golf, though it pleased the comic artists by marching sedately in tight knickers, deer-stalker and spats, overwhelmingly conquered the land. No place of any consequence now lacks one or more courses.

Golf news is of general interest and so hot is the pace of proficiency that a future champion can hardly hope for supreme honours unless he is 'a tiger' in his 'teens.

120 GOLF CHAMPIONSHIP AT WESTWARD HO!

121, 122   THE DOGS AND THE DERBY

The big championships are fought out in a hurly-burly of spectatorship and amid the roar of publicity. For every 'tiger' there are a myriad 'rabbits' playing golf in their leisure and boring their friends with the news, usually as false as wearisome, that they really are improving their game. Nor is golf only a middle-class pastime. There are many working-men's clubs and that greatest, kindliest and most modest of English golfers, J. H. Taylor, five times Open Champion, has fostered many of these and will foster more. Despite all the uproar of an up-to-date championship, with the wires chirping 'birdies' and screeching 'eagles' across the globe, golf will never be Wemblified utterly. Its real home is the green beside blue waters, with the yellow of the gorse for its favour.

In like manner fame and finance have seized upon lawn-tennis and turned the curate's pat-ball of the late Victorian cartoonists into the furious test of speed, skill and endurance which Wimbledon offers every June (119). So hot is the pace that no 'singles' champion, whatever his brilliance, can expect to retain supremacy for long; the combat, often running to five protracted 'sets' and lasting for two hours beneath a blazing sun, is even more exacting than the eighty minutes endured by a Rugby 'forward' in the ceaseless rush, maul and scrimmage of a hard-fought International. As a spectators' sport, lawn-tennis of the highest grade offers terrific tension; the crash of mighty service or a whistling side-line drive are thunderbolts indeed. But to a certain middle-class public the spectacle of Rugby football is quite as attractive as Association is to the millions (118). The mobility of our 'Rugger' is greater than that of the

American game, which is supposedly fiercer, though I doubt whether an American player who found himself, stripped of his helmet and his padding, in the middle of an English-Welsh International would regard his new environment as altogether namby-pamby. The spectacle of a great passing movement ribboning across the field or of weary forwards making one last drive in the growing dusk of a hard-fought afternoon has irresistible excitement; but, of course, one must know the game to appreciate the fine points and its rules are not simple. Furthermore attendance on these winter games is apt to be a chilly business, whereas to sit at Lord's Cricket Ground on a summer's day invites an exquisite lethargy even if the game be dull. The bird-music from St. John's Wood gardens tunes in with the crack of the bat and the white figures on the green make a charming pageant beneath a billowy sky. Thrills are scarce; this is a scene in which to saturate the senses, especially if one has access to the great Pavilion with its lovely gallery of old cricketing-pictures. One or two matches, especially that of Eton and Harrow, are fashionable occasions and provoke a feminine dress-parade. But to the true cricketer these irrelevant fripperies are merely vexatious.

A great deal was heard, during the nineteen-twenties, of Bright Young People who invented absurd parties, dashed about madly on motor treasure-hunts, drank and drugged and put up a Fifth-Georgian imitation of the First-Georgian Mohocks. They were a tiny set and the typical young man or woman of that time was far more likely to be spending leisure hours in austere, athletic ways. The idea of the Man About Town, the specimen 'Johnnie' of the 'nineties, had collapsed. To hang about

123   THE NORTHERN CLASSIC : A St. Leger Crowd at Doncaster

124, 125 THE PICTURES : Palace and Patrons

126, 127 SONGSTERS : Music-hall and Microphone

128   WELL-TO-DO: 1860

129   WELL-TO-DO: 1760

the West End visiting flashy lounge-bars, standing on
the promiscuous promenades of smart music-halls, and
coming home fuddled with the milk, as 'mashers' always
did in comic songs of the period, was no longer a young
gentleman's amusement. He had no notion of becoming
a podgy, puffy *roué* at forty. The clubs mainly patronised
by the Forsyte class had to attract new members by
installing squash-racket courts and swimming-baths. In
the suburbs there was a considerable development of
facilities for indoor exercise, such as table-tennis and
badminton, while artificial ice-rinks became popular.
But the slogan of 'Run, girls, run,' was no longer uttered
as a recipe for the production of pure souls above stout
calves. The young woman laced up her skating-boots
because she liked skating after a day on an office chair and,
if she had a pleasant partner, that was so much the better.
Exercise has become more general, less ethical, frankly
hedonistic.

The English are considerable gamblers—mainly, I
think, because they are told not to. If our politicians
would only legalise sweepstakes instead of vainly trying
to prevent them, there would first be a sudden spurt of
these dubious amusements and then a quick decline of
interest. But so long as there is a spice of guilt about them,
so long as an Englishman feels it 'up to him' to break
vexatious interferences with his right to spend his pocket-
money, so long will there be a ready market in smuggled
tickets for the big sweeps. Our betting laws are a tangle
of absurdity and public opinion despises them. In this
matter nobody is thought morally the worse for breaking
the law, which is a bad state of mind for a constitutional
country. Parliament, fearful of the small but well-

organised Puritan vote, fiddles with one compromise after another and, at a time when large and mainly agreed measures of social reconstruction are crowded out of its time-table, it can still find hours in which to arrange the calendar and the conditions of the greyhound racing tracks, which, in the last ten years, have multiplied rapidly. Their contests are held in the evening; they are put through more rapidly and are much cheaper to attend than horse-races. The working class 'follow' the latter by newspaper and may put in an occasional afternoon in the cheap enclosure at one of the big meetings. Horse-racing as a spectacle is largely an affair of specialist regulars, society folk, owners and professional backers; occasionally the larger public participates. Ascot is the annual garden-party of this sport and Epsom its bank-holiday. As a form of 'flutter' horse-racing continues to attract a good deal of money from all classes. But now 'the dogs' are snapping at the horses' heels in the race for popularity. The difference, perhaps, is mainly this: at the dog-track the man who must have a fling can see more for less and lose smaller sums at quicker intervals.

If the word 'recreation' is literally understood it may fairly include some notes on diet. Since the parts of an organism are interdependent, some gastric addition is pertinent to the discussion of a country's heart, if only by way of appendix. There can be no doubt that the English eat far less than they were wont to do. It is not merely that a craze for 'slimming' induced many young women to forgo all creams, fats, sugars and cereals and take instead to orange-juice, lettuces and biscuity breads; the general desire for fitness and observation of common-sense hygiene worked against heavy feeding. So also did the cost of food, which towered during the war to double its old price and took many years to descend. Many were thin of necessity, others of abnegation. The decline in quantitative standards of 'a good meal' may easily be traced by looking at the ceremonial menus of a social club over a series of years. The Victorian banquets were terrific affairs, divided by a water-ice or 'sorbet' to relieve the over-worked palate. Public dinners still provide plenty, but the old rate of absorption has notably slackened. Breakfast, again, used to be a great English meal, with porridge, fish, eggs and bacon or sausages all expected. When I was at Oxford a guest breakfast included butcher's meat and beer. Most hotels still provide a huge list of breakfast dishes, partly because they are incurably behind the times, and partly because most people pay for this mass of stuff and never eat a tenth of it. But enormous numbers of English people, who could easily afford to lay into eggs and bacon every morning, now start the day—and a hard-working day too—with coffee and toast and a little fruit.

Significant of new habits has been the recent popularity of sandwich-bars, where one perches on a high stool to eat slices of bread with rather messy heterogeneous contents. My personal opinion is that the smart sandwich-bar is more productive of indigestion than of nourishment; the 'snack' sounds cheap, but, when you reckon up what you have had, it turns out to be stupidly expensive. Your 'chicken and salad sandwich' may have contained about as much bird-meat as would fill a hollow tooth. While talking of chickens, it is worth remembering that the Victorians, when inviting to dinner, always

T

prevent some well-intentioned person from emptying a
pot of glue over the meat before it reaches you. I remember, at a sandwich-bar in New York, deliberately ordering tongue-sandwich in the hope that this would be left
to be its excellent self; but no, when it arrived, it was
soaked in mayonnaise. In England, when you ask for
tongue, you can get it unbedizened.

The stranger in England must find our sauceless,
uncreamed dishes extremely dull; his palate and his
digestion are both tuned up to higher standards. It is,
however, fair to argue that English sensibility is the finer;
we can taste food as it is; our neighbours can only taste
oil, paprika, garlic. The French have a lighter touch with
seasoning, but they depend much upon their sauces.
The absence of high relish is comparatively modern in
England. Tudor recipes abound in potent garnishes and
their habit of serving cloves with meat was outrageous.
The most repulsive food I have ever eaten was at a lunch
designed according to Elizabethan prescriptions. Turbot
and chicken, so admirable when simply boiled and roast,
were both canopied with irrelevant nastiness. English
cooking is a tribute to English grass; the better the meat,
the less need to disguise it. Continental cooking is a skil-
ful mask for tough meat; it can create the impression of
a tender *tournedos* by soaking it in oil, but the meat
comes out in a pappy, greasy state which is not to be
compared with the natural flavour of a good English
steak simply grilled. It must be admitted that a bad
English steak is terrible.

The weakness of English cooking lies in the tiresome
pretensions to foreign menus so common in country
hotels which insist on serving up five-shilling dinners

of tinned stuff with French names; also in our treatment of vegetables. The English cannot think of a meal which does not include potatoes and cabbage, usually sodden. The potato-obsession is a public nuisance. Potatoes are excellent stuffing for otherwise empty stomachs; they are joyous in spring and tolerable, at intervals, later on. But the eternal boiled potato is a bore beyond words; so is the eternal cabbage. Our winter vegetables include the admirable sea-kale, cauliflowers, spinach, leeks, carrots, turnips and celery, apart from preserved peas and beans. Yet to the average housewife vegetables mean boiled cabbage and in the average hotel cabbage and 'greens' make inevitable appearance, damp and depressing. I remember being in Devonshire in July; while I was buying cigarettes I heard a local grumbling to the tobacconist that his garden was overrun with peas and that he was sick of the sight of them. At lunch in the inn there was, of course, boiled cabbage and no alternative.

The English bake far better in the North than in the South. Tea is a great English meal, but in the Home Counties, should you call at one of the innumerable cottages labelled 'Teas,' the bread-stuff and the cakes are likely to be sad fare. North of the Trent, you begin to approximate to Scottish standards of scone and 'fancy bread'; a Yorkshire tea will almost certainly have excellent tea-cakes. It is a pleasing Yorkshire habit to load the table at all meals with all that the larder holds. Why not cheese, if you feel inclined, at breakfast and at tea? It is generally believed that the urban working class of England feed badly and wastefully and it is probably true that the Frenchwoman's ability to make a savoury dish from unpromising scraps is uncommon in English kitchens. The English prefer the teapot to the *pot-au-feu* and a few seconds with the tin-opener to a long vigil over a watched pan. The variety and quality of tinned food has risen so enormously of late that this practice has now a good deal to be said on its behalf. Good cooking is extremely hard work and the average woman in a poor family has usually had a full day's drudgery in and out of the house apart from her service of the oven; those who censure her cooking should first experience her workaday routine.

So toiling, rejoicing and frequently tin-opening, English life moves on. We are a patient people and understand the art of 'making do.' Sometimes a little less patience might have good results; the dawdling of the politicians over slum-conditions and depressed areas has been scandalous. Something is always going to be done and it actually would be done if Mrs. Smith of Fog Alley, Coketown, were less ready to 'make do,' if Mr. Smith were not so easily contented with football and the dog-track and if Miss Smith did not find such blissful escape at 'the pictures.' A frequent English answer to a query of "How are you?" is "Mustn't grumble." It shows that same nice temper which is to be observed at street-corners where Fascists and Communists orate side by side in a general atmosphere of banter. We crack jests where our Continental neighbours would be cracking skulls. The heart of England has fewer palpitations than has the similar organ of its neighbours; for that steadiness of pulse we have often reason to be thankful.

INDEX

(The numerals in italics denote the *figure numbers* of illustrations)

A Selected List of
BATSFORD BOOKS
relating to

Architecture, Fine and Decorative Art, Social History, The Countryside, Church Art, Interior Decoration, Design and Ornament, Crafts, etc.

Published by B. T. BATSFORD LTD

Booksellers and Publishers by Appointment to H.M. Queen Mary

15 North Audley Street, Mayfair
London, W 1

CONTENTS

NOTE.—This list comprises over 250 books on the subjects shown above from Batsford's main catalogue, in which are listed some 600 odd titles. It is intended to form a representative selection for the use of readers, but those interested in any particular subject should obtain the main catalogue (which will be sent post free on request), that comprises a much wider range of titles under every head. Fully illustrated prospectuses of most books can also be sent on request. Patrons are reminded that Batsford's new premises are at 15 North Audley Street, London, W.1, one minute from Oxford Street, on the main thoroughfare leading to Grosvenor Square, three minutes' walk from either Bond Street or Marble Arch Stations on the Central London Railway; there an immense stock of books, old and new, English and foreign, with prints, pictures, etc., can be inspected at leisure in the large and beautifully-fitted showrooms and gallery *Telephone Mayfair* 6118. *Cables: Batsfordia, London. Telegrams: Batsford, Audley, London.*

List G. 67m. 10/37.

THE ENGLISH GARDEN

By RALPH DUTTON. An expertly written account of the design and development of English gardens from medieval times to the XIXth century. Delightfully illustrated by about 120 photographs, largely specially taken by WILL F. TAYLOR, a selection from old manuscripts, prints and plans, and a coloured Frontispiece. Demy 8vo, cloth. 7s. 6d. net.

THE LAND OF WALES

By EILUNED and PETER LEWIS. A Pictorial Review of Welsh Scenery and Life, with chapters on the Countryside, the Towns, Sport, Religion, the Spirit of Wales, etc. Written by a Welsh brother and sister, both of whom have made names for themselves in literary spheres, the book forms the best introduction yet issued to Wales and the Welsh. With 130 superb photographic illustrations, and a colour Frontispiece. Demy 8vo, cloth. 7s. 6d. net.

THE OLD TOWNS OF ENGLAND

By CLIVE ROUSE, F.S.A. A Review of their Types and History, Features and Industries, including Cathedral Cities, Spas and Resorts, Market Towns, Scholastic and Church Centres, Sea Ports, etc. Illustrated by some 120 fine photographs of public and private buildings, picturesque byways, aerial views, etc. With coloured Frontispiece. Demy 8vo, cloth. 7s. 6d. net.

ENGLISH VILLAGE HOMES

By SYDNEY R. JONES, author of "Touring England," etc. With a Foreword by SIR W. BEACH THOMAS. An historical and comparative review of many types of Country Buildings, including the Farm, Cottage, Inn, Manor, Rectory, Cross, Lock-up, etc. Illustrated by some 130 fine photographs, many sketches and drawings and a coloured Frontispiece. Demy 8vo, cloth. 7s. 6d. net.

THE ENGLISH CASTLE

By HUGH BRAUN, F.S.A., A.R.I.B.A. A review of the origin, evolution and vicissitudes of medieval fortresses, with accounts of military engines, famous sieges, etc. Illustrated by a coloured Frontispiece and some 125 fine photographs of general and air views, features and details of the outstanding examples in England and Wales. Demy 8vo, cloth. 7s. 6d. net.

THE SEAS AND SHORES OF ENGLAND

By EDMUND VALE. An interesting account of the varied English and Welsh coastline, its Cliffs and Coves, Estuaries and Ports, Inlets and Harbours, including the Solway, the Irish Sea and St. George's Channel, the Severn Sea, the Atlantic, the English Channel and the North Sea. Illustrated by 130 photographs and a coloured Frontispiece. Demy 8vo, cloth. 7s. 6d. net.

THE ENGLISH COUNTRY HOUSE

By RALPH DUTTON. An historical and social review, tracing design and evolution from the Conquest to Victorian times, including Interior Decoration and Gardens. Illustrated by 130 fine Photographs of Medieval, Elizabethan, Stuart, Georgian, Classic and Neo-Gothic examples With coloured Frontispiece and numerous plans. Demy 8vo, cloth. 7s. 6d. net.

THE ENGLISH ABBEY: ITS LIFE & WORK IN THE MIDDLE AGES.

By FRED H. CROSSLEY, F.S.A. With a Foreword by the Rt. Hon. W. Ormsby-Gore, P.C., M.P. An informative review of Origins and Orders, the Working Staff of the Convent, the Buildings, Daily Round and Processions, Administration, Building Methods and Social Reactions. With 138 illustrations from photographs of interior and exterior views, features, etc., a map, numerous plans, and 3 coloured plates. Demy 8vo, cloth. 7s. 6d. net.

3

THE PARISH CHURCHES OF ENGLAND

By the Rev. J. C. Cox, LL.D. and CHARLES BRADLEY FORD. With a Foreword by the VERY REV, W, R, INGE, D.D., late Dean of St. Paul's. With Chapters on the Life and Services, the Evolution of Plan, Structural Design, Fittings and Furniture, and Local Varieties of Style. Including 135 fine photographic illustrations, also plans and drawings. With coloured Frontispiece. Second Edition. Demy 8vo, cloth. 7s. 6d. net.

THE CATHEDRALS OF ENGLAND

By HARRY BATSFORD, Hon. A.R.I.B.A., and CHARLES FRY, with a Foreword by HUGH WALPOLE. With an Introduction, followed by a description of each cathedral, its situation, history and architecture. Including 133 Illustrations from new photographs, a superb series, far in advance of anything yet produced, a colour Frontispiece, a complete series of uniform Scale Plans, Glossary, and 30 Line Sketches. Third edition, revised. Demy 8vo, cloth. 7s. 6d. net.

ENGLISH VILLAGES AND HAMLETS

By the Hon. HUMPHREY PAKINGTON, F.R.I.B.A., with a Foreword by E. V. KNOX ("Evoe"), Editor of *Punch*. A popular Pictorial Survey in 130 Photographic Illustrations of unspoilt varied examples from some 30 English counties, in stone, brick, plaster, half-timber and cob, including many unpublished Views, also Maps and 4 coloured Plates and 25 Pen Drawings by SYDNEY R. JONES. Second Edition, revised, with an Historical Introduction by G. M. YOUNG. Demy 8vo, cloth. 7s. 6d.

THE SPIRIT OF LONDON

By PAUL COHEN-PORTHEIM, author of "England the Unknown Isle." A series of original and brightly written chapters on Through the Centuries; Streets and their Life; Green London; Amusements and Night Life; Traditional London; and other subjects, with 144 selected photographic illustrations of London scenes and life, including a colour Frontispiece. Second Edition. Demy 8vo, cloth. 7s. 6d. net.

THE HEART OF ENGLAND

By IVOR BROWN. A Review, written with penetrating and sympathetic insight, on many aspects of present-day Life and Work, including Chapters on Seaport and Seaside; the Downs and the Moors; Country Matters; Markets and Mills; The Suburb; The Week-End; The Young Idea; Recreation. With 130 photographs and a coloured Frontispiece. Demy 8vo, cloth. 7s. 6d. net.

THE OLD INNS OF ENGLAND

By A. E. RICHARDSON, A.R.A., with a Foreword by Sir E. LUTYENS, R.A. A comprehensive survey of one of the most attractive features of English life. With a letterpress full of knowledge and robust humour. Illustrated by 130 fine photographs and 20 line drawings. Second Edition, revised. Demy 8vo, cloth. 7s. 6d. net.

THE COUNTRYMAN'S ENGLAND

By DOROTHY HARTLEY, author of "Here's England." An illustrated account of the various types of English country, the people and their occupations. Arranged under: Mountain and Moorland; Garden and Orchard Country; The Undulating Farmlands; Hill and Downland; Fens and Levels; Coast and Estuaries. With a superb series of 130 Photographic Illustrations, and a coloured Frontispiece. Demy 8vo, cloth. 7s. 6d. net.

THE SPIRIT OF IRELAND

By LYNN DOYLE. A bright, witty yet informative review of Dublin, the South-East Corner, Grasslands and County Towns, Cork and Kerry, Limerick and Clare, Galway and the North-West, Derry and Antrim, Belfast, etc. Illustrated by 138 superb unpublished Photographs of coast and mountains, islands, rivers, antiquities, cottages, towns, life in fairs, gatherings, sport, etc., forming an unrivalled pictorial survey. With 3 colour pictures by PAUL HENRY and HUMBERT CRAIG, and pen drawings and map by BRIAN COOK. Second Edition. Demy 8vo, cloth. 7s. 6d. net.

THE FACE OF SCOTLAND

A Pictorial Review of its Scenery: Hills, Glens, Lochs, Coast, Islands Moors, etc., with Old Buildings, Castles, Churches, etc. Including a brief review of Topography, History and Characteristics. By HARRY BATSFORD and CHARLES FRY, with a Foreword by JOHN BUCHAN (LORD TWEEDSMUIR). With 130 splendid photographic illustrations, a Frontispiece in colour, and numerous line drawings in the text. Third Edition. Demy 8vo, cloth. 7s. 6d. net.

THE HEART OF SCOTLAND

By GEORGE BLAKE, with a Foreword by ERIC LINKLATER. A companion and complement to "The Face of Scotland." Containing an account of the Land and its People, including a review of Highland Places, the True Lowlands, Black Country, a Tale of Four Cities, the Kirk and the People, the Fireside Clime, Sport, Institutions, Legends and Realities. Containing 130 superb Photographic Illustrations of Scenery and Life, Mountains Cities, Towns, Sport, etc. With a coloured Frontispiece by KEITH HENDER-SON, numerous drawings, and a map. Demy 8vo, cloth. 7s. 6d. net.

Further volumes in the "BRITISH HERITAGE" Series to appear shortly are:

ANCIENT ENGLAND. By EDMUND VALE.
A survey of the Ancient Monuments under the care of H.M. Office of Works and other public bodies.

THE OLD PUBLIC SCHOOLS OF ENGLAND. By JOHN RODGERS.

OLD ENGLISH COUNTRY LIFE. By H. E. BATES.

OLD ENGLISH CUSTOMS AND CEREMONIES. By E. DRAKE-CARNELL.

Price 7s. 6d. net each.

THE COLOURED COUNTIES

By CHARLES BRADLEY FORD. This volume, which is a revelation in illustrated book production, is the first work on the landscape of England to be illustrated solely by means of colour photography. There are 92 brilliant illustrations reproduced from Dufaycolor originals, and in these all the subtle nuances of the English landscape can for the first time be appreciated. Mr. Ford's vivid text presents an interesting and well-informed review of the beauties and antiquities of The Coloured Counties. Demy 8vo, cloth. With coloured jacket. 8s. 6d. net.

THE "FACE OF BRITAIN" SERIES

COTSWOLD COUNTRY

By H. J. MASSINGHAM. A vivid, first-hand account of LIMESTONE ENGLAND, from the Dorset Coast to Lincolnshire. Illustrated by 192 photographs, a map, a number of line drawings in the text and a colour Frontispiece. Demy 8vo, cloth, 7s. 6d. net.

NORTH COUNTRY

By EDMUND VALE. A Pictorial Survey of Northumberland, Durham, Cumberland, Westmorland, Lancashire and Yorkshire, rural and industrial, with an account of its life in town and country, ranging from the remote sheep-farming of the Pennines to the coal, steel and textile activities of the great manufacturing areas. A chapter on "No Man's Land" deals acutely with the problem of the Distressed Areas, while about 130 illustrations reveal every aspect of Northern life and scenery. With a Frontispiece in colour. Demy 8vo, cloth. 7s. 6d. net.

THE FACE OF IRELAND

By MICHAEL FLOYD. A vivid and human survey of Irish Scenery and Life. Splendidly illustrated by over 130 Photographs, for the most part specially taken by WILL F. TAYLOR. After a general Introduction, the country is treated under five broad divisions: Dublin, Wicklow and the South-East, Kerry and the South-West, Connemara and the Mid-West, Donegal and the North-East, the Six Counties, Central Ireland. The illustrations form, perhaps, the finest series ever devoted to their subject. Mr. PAUL HENRY contributes a colour Frontispiece. Demy 8vo, cloth. 7s. 6d. net.

THE HIGHLANDS OF SCOTLAND

By HUGH QUIGLEY. A graphic account of the Cairngorms, the Lower Grampians, the Far North-West, the West Coast, the Inner and Outer Hebrides and the Glencoe district. Illustrated by some 130 fine Photographs of mountains, lochs, seascapes, rivers, glens, woods, etc., by ROBERT M. ADAM. With coloured Frontispiece by W. DOUGLAS McLEOD, Maps, etc. Demy 8vo, cloth. 7s. 6d. net.

ENGLISH DOWNLAND

By H. J. MASSINGHAM, Author of "Wold Without End," "Downland Man," etc. A comprehensive review of the features, distinctive characteristics, antiquities, villages, etc., of the Chalk Country in England, including the Wiltshire Mass, the Berkshire Ridges, the Chilterns, the North and South Downs, etc. Illustrated by 130 fine photographs of general views, hill-scenes, panoramas, farms and fieldwork, cottages and churches, barrows, cromlechs, etc. With a Frontispiece in colour. Demy 8vo, cloth. 7s. 6d. net.

Forthcoming additions to the "FACE OF BRITAIN" Series include:

THE ISLANDS OF SCOTLAND. By H. M'DIARMID.

THE WELSH BORDER COUNTRY. By P. T. JONES. 7s. 6d. net each.

THE ISLANDS OF IRELAND

By THOMAS H. MASON. A racy, first-hand account, in text and pictures of their scenery, peoples, antiquities and primitive life, illustrated by some 140 reproductions of specially taken photographs of the Arans, Blaskets, Tory, Clare and other islands, including prehistoric forts, Christian antiquities, currachs, interiors, peasant types, etc. With a Frontispiece in colour. Large 8vo, cloth. 10s 6d. net.

THE BEAUTY OF BRITAIN

A new composite picture of the English, Welsh and Scottish countryside, under 14 divisions by various writers, with an Introduction by J. B. PRIESTLEY. Including the Coast, and Wales, by EDMUND VALE; the West Country by EDMUND BARBER; the Chalk Country by A. G. STREET; the Central Midlands by SIR W. BEACH THOMAS; Scotland, Lowlands and Highlands, by GEORGE BLAKE; and articles by other well-known writers. Containing 256 pages of text, with 130 splendid photographic pictures and a Frontispiece in colour. Second Edition, revised. Crown 8vo, cloth. 5s. net.

THE LEGACY OF ENGLAND

An Illustrated Survey of the Works of Man in the English Country: Farm, Village, Country House, Town, Church, Inn, Sport. With Introduction by EDMUND BLUNDEN and contributions by ADRIAN BELL, C. BRADLEY FORD, G. M. YOUNG, G. A. BIRMINGHAM, IVOR BROWN and BERNARD DARWIN. 256 pages, illustrated by 130 splendid photographs of examples from all parts. With colour Frontispiece. Crown 8vo, cloth. 5s. net.

NATURE IN BRITAIN

A Pictorial Review of our native wild Fauna and Flora, including Animals, Birds, Fishes and Water Life, Insects, Trees and Shrubs, and Flowers. With Introduction by HENRY WILLIAMSON, and contributions by FRANCES PITT, SETON GORDON, E. G. BOULENGER, C. BUSHBY, R. ST. BARBE BAKER and R. GATHORNE-HARDY. With 120 fine photographs and colour Frontispiece. Crown 8vo, cloth. 5s. net.

WORLD NATURAL HISTORY

By E. G. BOULENGER. Highly praised in an Introduction by H. G. WELLS, this book is at once the cheapest, most thorough and best illustrated work on its fascinating subject. Besides the 140 and more fine photographs there are a number of line-cuts in the 256 pages of text. Colour Frontispiece by PAUL ROBERT, and Jacket by BRIAN COOK. Demy 8vo, cloth. 7s. 6d. net.

SAILING AND CRUISING

By K. ADLARD COLES. An introductory handbook, with chapters on A First Sail, Half-Decked Boats, A Yacht's Gear, Coastal Navigation, A Short Cruise, Auxiliary Motors, etc. The illustrations include 104 photographs, 8 pages of marine designers' plans, numerous sketches and diagrams in the text, and a coloured Frontispiece and Jacket. Demy 8vo, cloth. 7s. 6d. net.

HUNTING ENGLAND

By SIR WILLIAM BEACH THOMAS, author of "Village England," etc. A survey of the sport and its chief grounds. With accounts of every leading pack and the country over which it hunts. Illustrated by 10 plates in colour (some double) from old paintings and prints by renowned artists, and over 100 subjects from photographs. Demy 8vo, cloth. 7s. 6d. net.

FARMING ENGLAND

By A. G. STREET. An illustrated survey of the regions, methods and problems of English agriculture, by an author who is himself a successful farmer. With chapters on The Warm and Wet South-West, London's Back-Garden, The Marches of Wales, East Anglia, etc. Illustrated by 134 photographs of farming people and farming methods in every part of England. With coloured Frontispiece and Jacket. Demy 8vo, cloth. 7s. 6d. net.

In Preparation:

RACING ENGLAND   BY PATRICK CHALMERS.

VICTORIAN PANORAMA

By PETER QUENNELL. This book presents the first pictorial survey of the Victorian Age to be compiled *solely through the medium of photography*. The 154 photographs begin as early as the 'Thirties and give a unique picture of Victorian life and manners. Mr. Quennell's text, which discusses such topics as The Beginnings of Photography, Low Life, Fashions, etc., provides a brilliant literary accompaniment to the illustrations. Demy 8vo, cloth, 7s. 6d. net.

MOVIES FOR THE MILLIONS

By GILBERT SELDES. An account of motion pictures in America and elsewhere, with a Foreword by Charlie Chaplin, and Mickey Mouse colour Frontispiece from an original specially drawn by WALT DISNEY. The 132 photographic illustrations present a miniature museum of the history of the industry and of the films it has produced. Demy 8vo, cloth. 7s. 6d. net.

CIRCUS PARADE

By JOHN S. CLARKE, Ex-Lion Tamer. A graphic first-hand survey and pictorial review of its fascination and thrills as seen in the acts and performers, with some account of the history of its past. Illustrated by some 120 vivid Photographs and Old Prints, and a Frontispiece in colour. Demy 8vo, cloth, with decorative photographic jacket. 7s. 6d. net.

MOTOR RACING AND RECORD BREAKING

By the well-known Record-holding Racer, CAPTAIN G. E. EYSTON, Author of "Flat Out," etc., and BARRÉ LYNDON, Author of "Circuit Dust," etc. An historical account of achievements and thrills in many countries, and the influence of racing on car design. With 110 vivid Photographic Illustrations of track and road racing in Europe and America, hill-climbing, risks and personalities, etc. Including a colour Frontispiece. Demy 8vo. 7s. 6d. net.

THE WAR OF THE GUNS

Experiences of a Battery Signaller on the Climax of the Western Front, 1917-19. By AUBREY WADE. With an Introduction by EDMUND BLUNDEN, Author of "Undertones of War," etc. A graphic and vividly written first-hand account of the last desperate fighting round Ypres, Messines, Passchendaele, the Cambrai front, the German break-through, Villers-Bretonneux, and the final advance. Illustrated by some 120 fine photographs, English and German, of trench fighting, artillery work, etc. With a coloured Frontispiece by SIR WILLIAM ORPEN, R.A. Demy 8vo. 7s. 6d. net.

ROYAL PROGRESS: ONE HUNDRED YEARS OF BRITISH MONARCHY, 1837-1937

By HECTOR BOLITHO. A fascinating account of the domestic history of the British Royal Family from the accession of Queen Victoria in 1837 to the Coronation of George VI in 1937. Profusely illustrated from old paintings and prints, and old and modern photographs, together with six plates in colour. Demy 8vo, cloth. 7s. 6d. net.

A Companion Volume to "The Spirit of London."

THE SPIRIT OF PARIS

By PAUL COHEN-PORTHEIM. This is one of the last works completed by the author before his lamented death. No one had a better eye for a city than Paul Cohen-Portheim, and in this book he has contrived one of the most delightful "portraits of places" he attempted—one that not only describes the architectural background, but gives a real insight into the lives, work, pleasures and activities of Parisians of every type. It is delightfully illustrated by over 120 Phtogoraphs. Demy 8vo, cloth. 7s. 6d. net.

BATSFORD'S "ART AND LIFE IN COLOUR" LIBRARY

In two sizes: (I) Quarto (II) Small Folio. (I) comprises BEAUTY OF TROPICAL BUTTERFLIES; WONDERS OF THE SEA: SHELLS; THE SEASONS OF THE YEAR in Masterpieces of Flemish Illumination; to be followed by TYPICAL MINERALS and ALPINE FLOWERS. Each contains 12 superb facsimile colour plates, reproduced regardless of expense, forming veritable works of art. With brief Introduction and text. Stiff covers, 5s. 6d. net. per volume.

II. PAINTING OF THE FAR EAST, chiefly Chinese, with some Japanese examples; the LANDSCAPES OF SWITZERLAND from views of a century ago; and WONDERS OF THE SEA: FISH, CORALS, MEDUSAL SQUIDS, Etc. With brief introductions and text. 7s. 6d. net per volume. These two sister series constitute an endeavour to represent some of the finest works of Nature and Art by the highest achievements of modern colour processes. No trouble or cost has been stinted to obtain most artistic facsimile results, which will appeal to all for their beauty and intrinsic interest. Copies in portfolio can be supplied for framing if wished. EARLY STAINED GLASS IN FRENCH CATHEDRALS Extra large volume 10s. 6d. net. The introductions on BUTTERFLIES and SHELLS are by Professor JULIAN HUXLEY, F.S.A. of the London Zoo; that of the volume on ILLUMINATION by Mr. FRANCIS KELLY, the writer on costume; that on FISH, by E. G. BOULENGER, Director of the Zoological Society's Aquarium; that on STAINED GLASS, by Dr. G. G. COULTON, the authority on medieval life; and to the volume on PAINTING OF THE FAR EAST by Mr. LAURENCE BINYON, the well-known authority on Oriental Art.

THE "ENGLISH LIFE" SERIES

THE MEDIEVAL STYLES OF THE ENGLISH PARISH CHURCH

By F. E. HOWARD, joint author of "English Church Woodwork," etc. A careful and informative account of the Evolution of Design, Features and Detail from early pre-Conquest days to the sixteenth century, including chapters on each Transitional Phase and on Methods of Studying a Parish Church. With 180 illustrations from photographs of exterior and interior views, etc., plans and mouldings. Large 8vo, cloth. 12s. 6d. net.

THE ENGLISH COUNTRYSIDE

By ERNEST C. PULBROOK. A Review of some of its Aspects, Features, and Attractions. With 126 Illustrations from Photographs, and a Pencil Frontispiece by A. E. NEWCOMBE. Large 8vo, cloth, gilt. 10s. 6d. net.

ENGLISH COUNTRY LIFE AND WORK

By ERNEST C. PULBROOK. Containing about 200 pages on Farmers, Old and New—Field-Work—Cottage Folk—The Village Craftsman—Religious Life, etc. With about 200 illustrations from photographs. Large 8vo, cloth, gilt. 12s. 6d. net.

OLD ENGLISH HOUSEHOLD LIFE

By GERTRUDE JEKYLL. Consisting of 17 sections on the Fireplace, Candle. light, the Hearth, the Kitchen, Old Furniture, Home Industries, Cottag- Buildings, Mills, Churchyards, etc. With 277 illustrations from photo- graphs, old prints and drawings. Large 8vo, cloth, gilt. 12s. 6d. net.

THE ENGLISH AT HOME

A graphic pictorial record from photographs specially taken by BILL BRANDT. With an Introduction by RAYMOND MORTIMER. Comprising 64 photogravure plates of typical scenes and Characters at Work and Play in Town and Country, including Racing, Betting, Mining, Children, rich and poor, Drinking, Bathing, City Life, Suburbs, a Garden Party, Tease high and low, Schools, Games, Sport, etc. 4to, boards, cloth back. 5s. net,

THE QUENNELLS "EVERYDAY LIFE" SERIES

A Graphic and Popular Survey of the Efforts and Progress of the Human Race now completed in 4 volumes. Crown 8vo, cloth. 5s. net each.

I. EVERYDAY LIFE IN THE OLD STONE AGE

Written and Illustrated by MARJORIE and C. H. B. QUENNELL. Containing 128 pages, including 70 Illustrations, and a coloured Frontispiece, from the Authors' Drawings, with a Chronological Chart. Second Edition, 5s. net.

II. EVERYDAY LIFE IN THE NEW STONE, BRONZE AND EARLY IRON AGES

Written and Illustrated by MARJORIE and C. H. B. QUENNELL. Containing 144 pages, with 90 original Illustrations from the Authors' Drawings, of Household Life, Agriculture, Pottery, Weapons, etc., including 2 plates in colour, a map, and a Chronological Chart. Second Edition. 5s. net.

III. EVERYDAY LIFE IN ROMAN BRITAIN

Written and Illustrated by MARJORIE and C. H. B. QUENNELL. Containing 128 pages, with over 100 original Illustrations from the Authors' Pen Drawings, of Cities and Camps, Villas, Ships, Chariots, Monuments, Costume, Military Life, Household Objects, Pottery, etc. Including 3 Colour Plates, Chart, and Map of Roads. Second edition, revised. 5s. net.

IV. LIFE IN SAXON, VIKING AND NORMAN TIMES

Written and Illustrated by MARJORIE and C. H. B. QUENNELL. Containing 128 pages, with over 100 original illustrations of Ships, Cooking, Metalwork, Buildings, Pottery, and Illuminated MSS., including 2 coloured plates, Historical Chart, etc. 5s. net.

THE QUENNELL "CLASSICAL SOCIAL LIFE" SERIES

"The Quennell books are likely to outlast some of the most imposing institutions of the post-war world. They are written with great scholarship and surprising lucidity. To speak in superlatives of this series is only justice, for seldom is there found such a unity between publisher, author, and illustrator as the Batsford books display."—*G.K.'s Weekly.*

VOL I. EVERYDAY THINGS IN HOMERIC GREECE

Written and Illustrated by MARJORIE and C. H. B. QUENNELL. Presenting a vivid picture based on the Social Life in the Iliad and Odyssey, etc. Illustrated by 70 Drawings by the Authors, after Vase Paintings and their own restorations. With Colour Frontispiece, Photographic Illustrations, Map, etc. Large 8vo, cloth. 7s. 6d. net.

VOL. II. EVERYDAY THINGS IN ARCHAIC GREECE

Written and Illustrated by MARJORIE and C. H. B. QUENNELL. An Account of Social Life from the close of the Trojan War to the Persian Struggle. Illustrated by 85 full-page and smaller Drawings by the Authors. With a coloured Frontispiece, a number of Photographic Illustrations, Map, etc. Large 8vo, cloth. 7s. 6d. net.

VOL. III. EVERYDAY THINGS IN CLASSICAL GREECE

Written and Illustrated by MARJORIE and C. H. B. QUENNELL. A vivid picture of Social Life in the Golden Age of Pericles, Socrates, Phidias, and Plato, 480-404 B.C. With Sections on Architecture; the Town and its Planning; Everyday Life; Sea Fights and Land Battles, etc. Illustrated by 83 Drawings specially made by the Authors. With coloured Frontispiece, Photographic Illustrations, Chart, Map, etc. Large 8vo, cloth. 8s. net.

THE QUENNELLS "EVERYDAY THINGS" SERIES

"In their volumes the authors have approached history from a new angle and in the process have revolutionised the teaching of it. In their hands it has become a live, vivid and picturesque subject, for they have breathed new life into old bones. Their methods are now widely and generally recognised and appreciated."—*Western Mail.*

A HISTORY OF EVERYDAY THINGS IN ENGLAND

Written and Illustrated by MARJORIE and C. H. B. QUENNELL. In Four Volumes. Medium 8vo, 8s. 6d. net each; also Vols. I and II, and III and IV, issued each pair bound in one volume, 16s. 6d. net.

VOL. I—EVERYDAY THINGS IN ENGLAND, 1066-1499

With 90 Illustrations, many full-page, and 3 Plates in colour. Second Edition, revised and enlarged, with additional illustrations. 8/6 net.

VOL. II—EVERYDAY THINGS IN ENGLAND, 1500-1799

With 4 coloured plates and 111 other illustrations from the Author's Drawings. Third Edition, revised and largely rewritten with many new illustrations. 8s. 6d. net.

The above 2 volumes are separately issued in parts for Schools and Class Teaching. Stiff paper covers. Price 3s. net each.

PART I.   ENGLAND UNDER FOREIGN KINGS (1066-1199).
PART II.   THE RISE OF PARLIAMENT (1200-1399).
PART III. THE HUNDRED YEARS' WAR (1400-1499).
PART IV.   THE AGE OF ADVENTURE (1500-1599).
PART V.   THE CROWN'S BID FOR POWER (1600-1699).
PART VI.   THE RISE OF MODERN ENGLAND (1700-1799).

VOL. III—EVERYDAY THINGS IN ENGLAND, 1733-1851

THE COMING OF THE INDUSTRIAL ERA. An Account of the Transition from Traditional to Modern Life and Civilization. Written and Illustrated by MARJORIE and C. H. B. QUENNELL. Tracing the Transformation of Agriculture, the coming of Steam Power, the application of Inventions, Trends in Social Life in Town and Country, Costume, Building, etc. Illustrated by 4 Coloured Plates, 120 full-page and smaller Drawings. Medium 8vo, art cloth. 8s. 6d. net.

VOL. IV.—EVERYDAY THINGS IN ENGLAND, 1852-1934

THE AGE OF PRODUCTION. An Account of Modern Life and Civilisation. Written and Illustrated by MARJORIE and C. H. B. QUENNELL. Treating of old and new methods regarding the Farmer and Food, Buildings, Town Planning, Slums, Schools, Furniture, Production and Distribution, Public Health, Transport, Social Life in Clothes, etc. Illustrated by 4 single and 3 double Plates in colour, 120 full-page and smaller Drawings specially prepared by the authors, and numerous Plates from Photographs and contemporary Prints. Medium 8vo, art cloth. 8s. 6d. net.

THE GOOD NEW DAYS

Things that Boys and Girls Should Know. By MARJORIE and C. H. B. QUENNELL. Demy 8vo, with coloured jacket. 6s. net.
A Series of bright informative talks about the fundamental factors of English Citizenship, present-day conditions and problems, and including comparisons with the past, in Agriculture, Towns and Suburbs, Trade and Finance, Production, Legislation, Leisure, Taxation, National Debt and Imprisonment, Armaments, etc., With historical summaries. Illustrated by numerous plans, diagrams, old prints and up-to-date photographs.

LIFE AND WORK OF THE ENGLISH PEOPLE THROUGH THE CENTURIES

A Pictorial Record from Contemporary Sources. By DOROTHY HARTLEY and MARGARET M. ELLIOT, B.A. (Lond.). Each volume is devoted to a century and contains about 150 pictures on 48 Plates, of Household Life, Industries, Building, Farming, Warfare, Transport, Children, Church Life, Gardens, etc. With an Introduction, Descriptive Notes, Chart, Analytical Index, Music, etc. Large (royal) 8vo, boards, lettered, or in portfolio with flaps, 3s. net, or in cloth, 3s. 6d. net per volume.

The Series has now been completed as follows:

I. SAXON TIMES TO 1300	IV. THE SIXTEENTH CENTURY
II. THE FOURTEENTH CENTURY	V. THE SEVENTEENTH CENTURY
III. THE FIFTEENTH CENTURY	VI. THE EIGHTEENTH CENTURY

Volumes I and II (Early Middle Ages), III and IV (Later Middle Ages), and V and VI (Renaissance) are also issued bound together in cloth to form 3 vols., 6s. net each; and Volumes I, II and III (Middle Ages), and IV, V and VI (Renaissance) are also bound in cloth to form 2 vols., at 9s. net each.

THE *"ESSENTIALS OF LIFE"* SERIES

By Lieut.-Colonel F. S. BRERETON, C.B.E. Bright, informative reviews of the Indispensable Things of Human Life. Each with 80 pages of text, and about 100 Illustrations in Line and Half-tone from Photographs, Drawings, Old Prints, etc., of Old and Modern Developments. Large crown 8vo, cloth. Cheaper reissue. 2s. 6d. net each.

CLOTHING: An Account of its Types and Manufacture. Contents: Materials — Spinning — Weaving — The Sewing Machine — A Morden Factory—Furs and Rubber—Leather and Tanning—Boots—Hats—Glovemaking—Dyeing and Cleaning—Pins—Needles—Buttons, etc.

TRAVEL: An Account of its Methods in Past and Present. Contents: Early Roads and Trading Routes—Coaching—The Steam Engine—Steamships and Railways—The Bicycle—The Petrol Engine—Air Travel—Postman—Wire or Wireless. With Illustrations of Coaches, Engines, Balloons, Aircraft, Ships, Steamers, etc.

ENGLAND IN TUDOR TIMES

An Account of its Social Life and Industries. By L. F. SALZMAN, M.A. F.S.A. With 138 pages of text, 64 full-page plates and numerous illustrations in the text. Demy 8vo, cloth. 5s.

TOURING LONDON

By W. TEIGNMOUTH SHORE. With an introduction by the Rt. Hon. John Burns, P.C. A Series of 4 Tours, covering the chief parts of Inner London, illustrated by 28 photographs, drawings and sketches, also a map of the City. Crown 8vo, cloth. 2s. 6d. net.

TOURING ENGLAND BY ROAD AND BY-WAY

A Popular Illustrated Guide, in a new form, to the Beauties of Rural England. By SYDNEY R. JONES. Comprising 20 Typical Tours under Five Divisions, with General Introduction and complete Map, Introduction to each District and specially drawn simplified Route Map of each Tour, which is described in detail, with finger-post reference to features, and buildings of Interest. Illustrated by 54 drawings and 50 photographs. Crown 8vo. 5s. net.

MASKS OF THE WORLD

A COMPREHENSIVE, COMPARATIVE SURVEY OF THE PRODUCTIONS OF MANY PEOPLES AND PERIODS. By JOSEF GREGOR, Director of the Theatrical Art Section, National Library, Vienna. With an Historical and Cultural Introduction and 255 Illustrations finely reproduced in collotype from specially taken Photographs, including 15 subjects in full colour. Comprising striking examples, with some complete robes, from primitive tribes in North and South America, Africa; the Far East; Ancient Greece and Rome; Renaissance France and Italy; and Modernist designers. Edition limited to 200 English copies. Small folio. Art linen, gilt. £6 6s. net.

MEDIEVAL COSTUME AND LIFE

An Historic and Practical Review. By DOROTHY HARTLEY. Containing 22 full-page Plates from Photographs of living Male and Female Figures in specially made Costumes from Medieval MSS., 20 Plates in Line from the Author's Drawings of practical Construction, Detail, Sketches, etc., and 40 Plates of some 200 Reproductions from Contemporary Manuscripts of scenes of Medieval life and work. Large royal 8vo, cloth. 12s. net.

A SHORT HISTORY OF COSTUME AND ARMOUR, CHIEFLY IN ENGLAND, 1066-1800

By F. M. KELLY and RANDOLPH SCHWABE, Principal of the Slade School of Fine Art. Royal 8vo, cloth, gilt. 25s. net. Or in 2 volumes:

I. THE MIDDLE AGES, 1066-1485. With Sections on Civilian Dress, "Shirts," "Shapes," Houppelandes and Burgundian Modes Armour. Illustrated by 4 Plates in colours and gold, over 100 Pen Drawings and 32 Photographic Plates. Royal 8vo, cloth, gilt. 13s. net.

II. THE RENAISSANCE, 1485-1800. With Sections on Puff and Slashes, The Spanish Trend, "Cavalier" and French Modes, the Heyday and Decline of Powder, Armour, etc. Illustrated by 5 Plates (3 double) in colours and gold, over 100 Pen Drawings and 36 Photographic Plates of 58 Reproductions. Royal 8vo, cloth, gilt. 13s. net.

HISTORICAL COSTUME

A Chronicle of Fashion in Western Europe, 1490-1790. By FRANCIS M. KELLY and RANDOLPH SCHWABE. Containing the chief characteristics of Dress in each century. Illustrated by some hundreds of full-page and text Sketches from original sources by RANDOLPH SCHWABE of typical groups, figures and details. Including 7 Plates specially reproduced in colour, and 70 Photographic reproductions of Pictures, Portraits, Scenes, etc. Second Edition revised and enlarged. Large royal 8vo, cloth, gilt. 25s. net.

SCRAPBOOK

By CECIL BEATON. A highly entertaining Farrago, containing more than 350 photographs, paintings and drawings (reproduced in colour and monochrome) of ballet décors, film stars, society figures, actresses, etc., and a series of articles on Hollywood, The Russian Ballet, Taking Photographs, Fashions, etc. Medium 8vo, cloth, 21s. net. De Luxe Edition, limited to 150 signed copies, and bound in Parchment Vellum, £3 3s. net.

SHAKESPEARE'S "ROMEO AND JULIET"

With designs for Costumes and Stage Settings by OLIVER MESSEL. A beautiful edition of this famous tragedy, decoratively printed, containing 96 pages of text, 8 colour and 32 monochrome collotype Plates of the designs specially made for the Metro-Goldwyn-Mayer Film Production. Special limited edition. Demy 4to, decorative cloth and colour jacket. 21s. net.

A HISTORY OF ARCHITECTURE on the Comparative Method for the Student, Craftsman and Amateur

By Sir Banister Fletcher, PP.R.I.B.A., F.S.A. Ninth Edition, completely rewritten. Containing over 1,000 pages, with about 4,000 Illustrations (1,560 recently added and nearly 2,000 reproduced larger) from Photographs of Buildings and from specially arranged comparative Drawings of Structures, Plans, Detail and Ornament. Royal 8vo, cloth, gilt. £2 2s. net.

"A wonderful storehouse of accurate information enriched by an amazing wealth of illustrations. Author and publisher alike are to be congratulated on a remarkable achievement."—*The Journal of the Royal Institute of British Architects.*

BATSFORD'S "HISTORICAL ARCHITECTURE LIBRARY
of Standard Textbooks on Classic and Renaissance Architecture

ARCHITECTURE OF GREECE AND ROME

By W. J. Anderson and R. Phene Spiers. Now reissued in two volumes, obtainable separately, revised and much enlarged. Medium 8vo, cloth, gilt. 21s. net each volume, or £2 the two.

I. ARCHITECTURE OF ANCIENT GREECE. Rewritten, remodelled and much enlarged by William Bell Dinsmoor, Professor of Architecture at Columbia University, New York, and the American Academy at Athens. With over 200 Illustrations in Collotype, half-tone and line.

II. ARCHITECTURE OF ANCIENT ROME. Revised and rewritten by Thomas Ashby, LL.D., Late Director of the British School at Rome. With about 200 Illustrations in half-tone and line.

BYZANTINE ARCHITECTURE AND DECORATION

By J. Arnott Hamilton, M.A., author of "The Churches of Palermo," etc. A careful, scholarly and thorough account of the development and character of constructional methods and decoration, and types of extant buildings in Constantinople, Greece, the Balkans, Cyprus, Armenia, Italy, etc. With coloured Frontispiece and 120 Photographic Illustrations of exteriors and interiors, Constructional Diagrams, Carving, Details, etc., and numerous Line Drawings. Medium 8vo, cloth, gilt. 18s. net.

ARCHITECTURE OF THE RENAISSANCE IN ITALY

By William J. Anderson, A.R.I.B.A. Revised and Enlarged, with an additional Chapter on Baroque and later work, by Arthur Stratton, F.S.A., F.R.I.B.A. With 80 Plates, including 16 in Collotype, and 120 Illustrations in the text. Medium 8vo, cloth, gilt. 21s. net.

ARCHITECTURE OF THE RENAISSANCE IN FRANCE

By W. H. Ward, M.A., F.R.I.B.A. Revised and Enlarged by Sir John W. Simpson, K.B.E., PP.R.I.B.A. In two volumes, obtainable separately. Medium 8vo, cloth, gilt. 21s. net, each volume, or £2 for the two.
IV. THE EARLY RENAISSANCE (1495-1640). With 259 Illustrations.
V. THE LATER RENAISSANCE (1640-1830). With 214 Illustrations.

The following new volume in the Historical Architecture Library will appear shortly:
A HISTORY OF SPANISH ARCHITECTURE from the Earlist Times to the Nineteenth Century. By Bernard Bevan, M.A. Profusely illustrated by photographs, drawings and plans. Medium 8vo, cloth. Price 21s. net (approx.).

A SHORT CRITICAL HISTORY OF ARCHITECTURE

By H. HEATHCOTE STATHAM, F.R.I.B.A. Second Edition, revised and enlarged by G. MAXWELL AYLWIN, F.R.I.B.A. Containing 600 pages and 750 Illustrations from Photographs, Drawings, Plans, Prints, etc., with Chronological Charts and Glossary. Demy 8vo, cloth, gilt. 16s. net.

Also supplied in 3 parts, cloth, gilt. 6s. net each.

I. Architecture of Antiquity and the Classic Ages
II. Byzantine, Romanesque and Saracenic Styles
III. The Middle Ages and the Renaissance to Modern Times.

" Within the limits of its size and price it is the most valuable handbook that has appeared in English for those who wish to understand the architecture of the past." —*The Architect.*

THE STORY OF ARCHITECTURE

From the Earliest Ages to the Present Day. By P. LESLIE WATERHOUSE, F.R.I.B.A. With 131 Illustrations of the great buildings of all time from Photographs and Drawings, and many Diagrams in the text of Plans, Views and features. F'cap 8vo, boards. 6s. net.

THE STORY OF ARCHITECTURE IN ENGLAND

By WALTER H. GODFREY, F.S.A., F.R.I.B.A. A popular illustrated account, in which the aims and methods of Architectural Design are simply explained, and linked up with the social life of the time. In Two Parts: I. Early and Medieval, to 1500, chiefly Churches; II. Renaissance, 1500-1800, chiefly Houses. Demy 8vo, cloth. 6s. 6d. net per part.

I. PRE-REFORMATION, THE PERIOD OF CHURCH BUILDING
Illustrated by 133 photographs and drawings. 6s. 6d. net.
II. RENAISSANCE, THE PERIOD OF HOUSE BUILDING
Illustrated by 150 photographs and drawings. 6s. 6d. net.

ENGLISH GOTHIC CHURCHES

THE STORY OF THEIR ARCHITECTURE. By CHARLES W. BUDDEN, M.A. A simple informative account of the Planning, Design, and Details of Parish Churches, Cathedrals, etc., 1066-1500, including Chapters on Local Building, Towers, Spires, Ornaments, etc. Illustrated by 53 Plans and Line Diagrams, and 40 Photographic Plates of 80 Views and Details, including a County List of the chief Churches worth seeing. Crown 8vo, cloth, 5s. net.

ENGLAND'S GREATER CHURCHES

A Pictorial Record with an Introduction and Descriptive Notes by C. B. NICOLSON. Containing 100 Illustrations of general and detail views, exterior and interior, of Cathedrals, Abbeys, Collegiate Churches and Chapels, etc. Square 8vo, 4to cloth, pictorial sides. 3s. 6d. net.

THE ENGLISH HOME FROM CHARLES I TO GEORGE IV

By J. ALFRED GOTCH, F.S.A. A Review of the development of House Building, Decoration and Garden Design from Early Stuart times to the commencement of the XIXth Century. Containing 300 Illustrations, showing Decoration, Panelling, Gardens, Iron and Lead Work, Street Lay-outs, Shop Fronts, etc., etc. Large 8vo, cloth, gilt. 30s. net.

THE GROWTH OF THE ENGLISH HOUSE

A short History of its Design and Development from 1100 to 1800 A.D. By J. ALFRED GOTCH, F.S.A., PP.R.I.B.A. Containing 300 pages, with over 150 Illustrations from Photographs, and many pictures in the text from Measured Drawings, Sketches, Plans, and Old Prints. Second Edition, revised and enlarged. Large crown 8vo, cloth, gilt. 12s. 6d. net.

THE DOMESTIC ARCHITECTURE OF ENGLAND DURING THE TUDOR PERIOD

Illustrated in a Series of Photographs and Measured Drawings of Country Houses, Manor Houses and Other Buildings. By THOMAS GARNER and ARTHUR STRATTON, F.R.I.B.A. Second Edition, Revised and Enlarged, comprising 210 Plates, mostly full-page, finely reproduced in Collotype, and 250 pages of Historical and Descriptive Text, including 462 Illustrations of Additional Views, Plans, Details, etc., from photographs and drawings, making a total of over 800 Illustrations in all. In two volumes, small folio, buckram, gilt. £9 9s. net the set. (The volumes cannot be obtained separately but *the set can be purchased by instalments*.)

THE SMALLER ENGLISH HOUSE FROM 1660-1840

By A. E. RICHARDSON, A.R.A., F.R.I.B.A., and HAROLD DONALDSON EBERLEIN, B.A. Treating of the Characteristics and Periods of Style; the Evolution of Plan; Materials and Craftsmanship: Roofing, Windows, Ironwork, Fireplaces, Staircases, Wall Treatment, Ceilings. With over 200 illustrations from photographs and drawings. Demy 4to, cloth. 15s. net.

THE OLD HALLS AND MANOR HOUSES OF NORTH-AMPTONSHIRE

By J. ALFRED GOTCH, M.A., F.S.A., F.R.I.B.A. With full Historical Introduction and descriptive text, and 100 plates of some 150 illustrations from photographs, original drawings and old prints, comprising Interior and Exterior Views, Features, Plans, Details and Gardens. Crown 4to, cloth. 21s. net.

THE STYLES OF ENGLISH ARCHITECTURE

A SERIES OF COMPARATIVE WALL OR LECTURE DIAGRAMS. For Schools, Teachers, Students, etc. By ARTHUR STRATTON, F.S.A., F.R.I.B.A.

Series I: THE MIDDLE AGES (Saxon Times to the Start of the Tudor Period). Consisting of 13 diagrams, 20in. by 30in. 13s. net on stout paper, or 32s. net mounted on linen.

Series II: THE RENAISSANCE (Tudor, Elizabethan, Stuart, and Georgian Periods). Comprising 12 diagrams. 12s. net paper, or 30s. net mounted.

An Introductory Handbook to each series is issued, containing reduced reproductions of all the plates, and an outline account of each style with further illustrations. Paper covers 1s. 6d. net; cloth 2s. 6d. net each.

GEORGIAN ENGLAND (1700-1830)

A Review of its Social Life, Arts and Industries. By Professor A. E. RICHARDSON, A.R.A., F.R.I.B.A. Containing sections on the Social Scene, Navy, Army, Church, Sport, Architecture, Building Crafts, the Trades, Decorative Arts, Painting, Literature, Theatres, etc. Illustrated by 200 subjects from Photographs and contemporary Prints, Engravings and Drawings. With 54 Line Text Illustrations, and a Colour Frontispiece. Medium 8vo, cloth, gilt. 21s. net.

THE XVIIIth CENTURY IN LONDON

An Account of its Social Life and Arts. By E. BERESFORD CHANCELLOR. Containing 280 pages, with 192 illustrations from prints and contemporary drawings and a Frontispiece in colour. 4to, cloth, gilt. 15s. net.

LIFE IN REGENCY AND EARLY VICTORIAN TIMES

An Account of Social Life in the days of Brummel and D'Orsay (1800-1843). By E. BERESFORD CHANCELLOR. With numerous illustrations from rare prints and original drawings. Large 8vo, cloth, gilt. 12s. 6d. net.

FORM AND DESIGN IN CLASSIC ARCHITECTURE

By ARTHUR STRATTON, F.S.A., F.R.I.B.A. Presenting in 80 Plates from Measured Drawings, 600 motives of Façades, Halls, Colonnades, Staircases, etc., selected from fine representative buildings shown in Plan, Elevation and Section. 4to, cloth, gilt. 28s. net.

"This beautiful book is a most welcome addition to the library of architecture. Nothing could be simpler or more logical; yet it gives us an idea of the variety, complexity, and beauty of this classic architecture."—*Journal of the Royal Institute of British Architects.*

THE ORDERS OF ARCHITECTURE

GREEK, ROMAN, and RENAISSANCE; with examples of their historic APPLICATION IN ITALIAN, FRENCH, ENGLISH, and AMERICAN BUILDINGS. By ARTHUR STRATTON, F.S.A. With an Introduction by A. TRYSTAN EDWARDS, A.R.I.B.A. Illustrated in a series of 80 plates from specially prepared drawings, including a complete series of Vignola's Orders, and rendered examples of French, Italian, and English buildings. With full historical and practical notes. 4to, bound in cloth, gilt, or in portfolio, 21s. net; or in 3 parts: CLASSIC, ITALIAN, and APPLICATIONS, cloth 8s. net each.

RENAISSANCE PALACES OF NORTHERN ITALY

(With some Buildings of Earlier Periods). From the XIIIth to the XVIIth Centuries. Edited by PROFESSOR DR. ALBRECHT HAUPT, in 3 vols., each containing 160 full-page Plates in Collotype from specially taken Photographs or Measured Drawings. With full text. Vol. I, TUSCANY, FLORENCE, PISA, SIENA, MONTEPULCIANO, LUCCA, PISTOIA, etc.; Vol. II, VENICE, including also VERONA, MANTUA, VICENZA, and PADUA; Vol. III, GENOA, including also BOLOGNA, FERRARA, MODENA, MILAN, TURIN, PAVIA, BERGAMO, BRESCIA, etc. Small folio, cloth, £2 15s. net each volume, or the set of 3 for £7 10s. net.

EARLY CHURCH ART IN NORTHERN EUROPE

With special Reference to Timber Construction and Decoration. By Professor JOSEF STRZYGOWSKI, Author of "Origin of Christian Church Art," etc. Dealing with PRE-ROMANESQUE ART OF THE CROATIANS; WOODEN ARCHITECTURE IN EASTERN EUROPE; HALF-TIMBER CHURCHES IN WESTERN EUROPE; THE MAST CHURCHES OF NORWAY; ROYAL TOMBS IN SCANDINAVIA. With 190 Illustrations. Royal 8vo, cloth, gilt. 21s. net.

ART IN THE LIFE OF MANKIND

A Survey of its Achievements from the Earliest Times. By ALLEN W. SEABY. Planned in a series of concise volumes, each containing about 80 pages of text, with about 70 illustrations from the author's drawings, and a series of 16 photographic plates. Crown 8vo, cloth. 5s. net per volume.

I. A GENERAL VIEW OF ART: ITS NATURE, MEANING, PRINCIPLES AND APPRECIATION. II. THE ART OF ANCIENT TIMES (EGYPT, CHALDÆA, ASSYRIA, PERSIA, and other lands). III. GREEK ART. IV. ROMAN AND BYZANTINE ART.

These volumes are designed to serve as an Introduction to the Appreciation and Study of Art in general. They are simply written and fully illustrated.

A SHORT HISTORY OF ART

From Prehistoric times to the Nineteenth Century. Translated from the French of Dr. ANDRÉ BLUM. Edited and Revised by R. R. TATLOCK. Illustrated by 128 full-page Photographic Plates, comprising about 350 examples of the finest Painting, Sculpture, Architecture, and Decorative Art of Early, Classic, Byzantine, Gothic, Renaissance, and Recent Times. Medium 8vo, gilt. 12s. 6d. net.

THE CHEAP COTTAGE AND SMALL HOUSE

By GORDON ALLEN, F.R.I.B.A. New Edition, remodelled and enlarged, containing over 150 Illustrations from Drawings and Photographs of Cottages and their Plans, Housing Schemes, etc., from typical Designs. Medium 8vo, cloth. 8s. 6d. net.

A BOOK OF BUNGALOWS AND MODERN HOMES

A series of Typical Designs and Plans. By CECIL J. H. KEELEY, F.S.I., A.R.San.I., Architect. Comprising 36 Designs, with large scale Plans, Brief Descriptions and Estimated Cost, including some two-Storey Houses, Frontispiece in colour, Interior Views, Photographic Plates, etc. Large 8vo, cloth, 7s. 6d. net.

MODERN THEATRES AND CINEMAS

By P. MORTON SHAND. A series of 80 plates giving over 100 examples of exteriors, interiors, foyers, vestibules, lighting, mural decoration, details, etc., of Theatres and Cinemas in the modern post-war style in France, Germany, England, Scandinavia, Italy, America, etc. Containing reproductions of the work of such architects as Margold, Kaufmann, Siclis, Gropius, Lipp, Ionides, Sauvage, de Soissons, Wilms, Mendelsohn, etc. Containing in addition numerous plans, elevations, sections in the text. Cr. 4to, art canvas. 15s. net.

BRITISH ARCHITECTS OF THE PRESENT DAY

By PROFESSOR C. H. REILLY, M.A., F.R.I.B.A., late Director of the Liverpool School of Architecture. An Account of Twelve Typical Figures, their Careers and Work, including Professor Adshead, Robert Atkinson, Sir Herbert Baker, Sir R. Blomfield, A. J. Davis, Sir E. Guy Dawber, Clough Williams-Ellis, W. Curtis Green, H. V. Lanchester, Sir E. L. Lutyens, Sir Giles Gilbert Scott and Walter Tapper. With 130 illustrations of well-known buildings, and including 12 portraits. Large 8vo, cloth. 7s. 6d. net.

ARCHITECTURAL DRAWING

By G. GORDON HAKE, F.R.I.B.A., and E. H. BUTTON, Architects. An Introductory Treatise for Architects and Students on work of every type and in every medium. With 96 pages, 16 pages of Half-tone Illustrations and 90 Line Illustrations. Cheaper reissue. 8vo, cloth. 7s. 6d. net.

GARDENS IN THE MAKING

By WALTER H. GODFREY. A simple Guide to the Planning of a Garden. With upwards of 70 Illustrations of Plans, Views, and various Garden Accessories. Crown 8vo, cloth 7s. 6d. net.

THE ART AND CRAFT OF GARDEN MAKING

By THOMAS H. MAWSON, assisted by E. PRENTICE MAWSON, Fifth Edition, Revised and Enlarged. Containing 440 pages, illustrated by 544 Plans, Sketches and Photographs, and 5 colour Plates. Including Site, Entrances, Gates, Avenues, Terraces, Beds, Pergolas, Treillage, Rock and Water, Greenhouses, etc., etc., and list of Shrubs and Trees. Small folio, buckram, gilt. £3 15s. net.

SPANISH GARDENS

By Mrs. C. M. VILLIERS-STUART. With 6 plates in colour from the author's original water-colour drawings, 80 pages of reproductions of gardens, statuary, cascades, garden features, etc., from photographs, and numerous illustrations in the text from old engravings, pen drawings, etc. Small royal 8vo, cloth. 25s. net.

ENGLISH CHURCH SCREENS

A comprehensive Review of their Evolution and Design, including Great Roods, Tympana and Celures in Parish Churches during Medieval and Renaissance Times. By AYMER VALLANCE, M.A., F.S.A., author of "Crosses and Lychgates," "The Old Colleges of Oxford," etc. Illustrated by some 300 reproductions of typical examples, detail, carving, etc., from photographs, measured drawings and sketches, including many no longer extant and a series in colour from water-colour drawings. 4to, cloth. 25s. net.

OLD CROSSES AND LYCHGATES

A Study of their Design and Craftsmanship. By AYMER VALLANCE, M.A., F.S.A. With over 200 fine Illustrations from special Photographs, Old Prints, and Drawings. Crown 4to, art linen. 12s. 6d. net.

ENGLISH CHURCH WOODWORK AND FURNITURE

A Study in Craftsmanship from A.D. 1250-1550. By F. E. HOWARD and F. H. CROSSLEY, F.S.A. Illustrating, in over 480 examples from Photographs, the Development of Screens, Stalls, Benches, Font-Covers, Roofs, Doors, Porches, etc., with details of the Carved and Painted Decoration, etc., etc. Crown 4to, cloth, gilt. 25s. net.

ENGLISH CHURCH MONUMENTS, A.D. 1150-1550

By F. H. CROSSLEY, F.S.A. A survey of the work of the old English craftsmen in stone, marble, and alabaster. Containing over 250 pages, with upwards of 350 Illustrations, from special Photographs and Drawings. Crown 4to, cloth, gilt. 21s. net.

ENGLISH CHURCH FITTINGS AND FURNITURE

By the Rev. J. C. COX, LL.D., F.S.A. A Popular Survey, treating of Churchyards, Bells, Fonts and Covers, Pulpits, Lecterns, Screens, Chained Books, Stained Glass, Organs, Plate and other features of interest. With upwards of 250 Illustrations from Photographs and Drawings. 8vo, cloth, gilt. 12s. 6d. net.

ANCIENT CHURCH CHESTS AND CHAIRS IN THE HOME COUNTIES ROUND GREATER LONDON

By FRED ROE, R.I., R.B.C. A survey of the finest of these survivals of ancient craftsmanship by the leading authority on the subject. With 95 illustrations, many full page, from drawings by the author and from photographs. Demy 4to, cloth, gilt. 12s. 6d. net.

OLD ENGLISH FURNITURE: THE OAK PERIOD, 1550-1630

Its Characteristics, Features, and Detail from Tudor Times to the Regency. By J. T. GARSIDE. Containing 30 plates reproduced from the author's drawings illustrating about 400 details of Table Legs; Bedposts; Corbels; Friezes; Capitals; Panels; Inlay Motives; Metal Fittings, etc. Including also drawings of type-pieces of the period and 20 photographic illustrations. With an Historical Introduction, etc. 8vo, cloth. 7s. 6d. net.

ENGLISH INTERIORS FROM SMALLER HOUSES OF THE XVIITH to XIXTH CENTURIES, 1660-1820

By M. JOURDAIN. Illustrating the simpler type of Design during the Stuart, Georgian, and Regency Periods. Containing 200 pages, and 100 Plates, comprising 200 Illustrations, from Photographs and Measured Drawings of Interiors, Chimney-pieces, Staircases, Doors, Ceilings, Panelling, Metalwork, Carving, etc. With descriptive text. 4to, cloth, gilt. 15s. net.

BATSFORD'S LIBRARY OF DECORATIVE ART

In 4 volumes forming an attractive Series of remarkable scope and completeness. Each volume has an extensive series of plates, and is a complete guide to the work of its Period. The volumes are remarkable for the beauty and number of their illustrations, the simplicity and clearness of their arrangement. The complete series is published at prices amounting to £10, but is supplied for the present at the special price of £9 net.

"These handsome volumes with their extremely fine and copious illustrations provide a full survey of English Furniture and Decoration."—*The Times.*

VOL. I. DECORATION AND FURNITURE IN ENGLAND DURING THE EARLY RENAISSANCE, 1500-1660

An Account of their Development and Characteristic Forms during the Tudor, Elizabethan and Jacobean Periods, by M. JOURDAIN. Containing about 300 pages, and over 200 full-page Plates (with Coloured Frontispiece and some in Photogravure), including over 400 Illustrations, from specially made Photographs and Measured Drawings, and from Engravings. Folio (size 14 x 10½ in.), cloth, gilt. £2 10s. net.

VOL. II. FURNITURE IN ENGLAND FROM 1066 TO 1760

By FRANCIS LENYGON. A Survey of the Development of its Chief Types. Containing 300 pages with over 400 Illustrations, from special Photographs, together with 5 in colour. Second Edition, revised with many new Illustrations. Folio (14 in. x 10½ in.), cloth, gilt. £2 10s. net.

VOL. III. DECORATION IN ENGLAND FROM 1640 TO 1770

By FRANCIS LENYGON. A Review of its Development and Features. Containing 300 pages with over 350 Illustrations, of which 133 are full-page, from special Photographs, and 4 in colour. Second Edition, Revised and Enlarged. Folio (14 in. x 10½ in.), cloth, gilt. £2 10s. net.

VOL. IV. DECORATION AND FURNITURE IN ENGLAND DURING THE LATER XVIIITH CENTURY, 1760-1820

An Account of their Development and Characteristic Forms, by M. JOURDAIN. Containing about 300 pages, with over 180 full-page Plates (a selection in Collotype), including over 400 Illustrations, from specially made Photographs and Measured Drawings, and from Engravings. Folio (size 14 x 10½ in.), cloth, gilt. £2 10s. net.

OLD ENGLISH FURNITURE FOR THE SMALL COLLECTOR: ITS HISTORY, TYPES AND SURROUNDINGS

By J. P. BLAKE and A. E. REVEIRS-HOPKINS. Containing 150 pages with about 130 illustrations from photographs, old prints and pictures, original designs, Ornaments, etc. The book is planned as a handy guide to the simpler types of old furniture which appeal to the collector of average means. Med. 8vo. 12s. 6d. net.

ENGLISH PLASTERWORK OF THE RENAISSANCE

By M. JOURDAIN. Comprising over 100 full-page plates of Elizabethan, Stuart, Georgian, and Adam ceilings, friezes, overmantels, panels, ornament, detail, etc., from specially taken photographs and from measured drawings and sketches. Demy 4to, cloth. 15s. net.

A HISTORY OF ENGLISH WALLPAPER

From the Earliest Period to 1914. By ALAN VICTOR SUGDEN and JOHN LUDLAM EDMONDSON. With 70 Plates in colour and 190 Illustrations, including many full-page Specimens of Wallpapers from the XVIth to the XXth Centuries. Large 4to, art buckram, gilt. £3 3s. net.

OLD PEWTER: Its Makers and Marks

A Guide for Collectors, Connoisseurs, and Antiquaries. By Howard Herschel Cotterell, First Vice-President of the Society of Pewter Collectors. Containing about 500 pages, with 64 Plates of 200 Specimens of British Pewter, dated and described, and a List of 5,000 to 6,000 Pewterers, with Illustrations of their Touches and Secondary Marks, Facsimile Reproductions of existing Touch-Plates, and Text Illustrations. Cheaper reissue. Demy 4to, cloth, gilt. £3 3s. net.

OLD SILVER OF EUROPE AND AMERICA

From Early Times to the XIXth Century. By E. Alfred Jones. A Survey of the Old Silver of England, America, Austria, Belgium, Canada, Czechoslovakia, Denmark, France, Germany, Holland, Hungary, Ireland, Italy, Norway, Poland, Portugal, Russia, Scotland, Spain, Sweden, Switzerland, etc. With a Chapter on Spurious Plate and 96 Photogravure Plates, comprising 537 subjects. Cheaper reissue. Crown 4to, art canvas, 18s. net.

CHINESE JADE

A Comprehensive Introductory Review for Collectors and Students. By Stanley Charles Nott. With an Introduction by Sir Cecil Harcourt Smith, K.C.V.O., formerly Director of the Victoria and Albert Museum. Dedicated by permission to Her Gracious Majesty Queen Mary. With a full series of illustrations of the finest products of the art of all periods on 40 plates in facsimile colour and 112 from photographs, including examples belonging to H.M. the King, H.M. Queen Mary, H.R.H. the Duke of Kent, and other English and Continental royal, private and public collections. Small 4to, cloth, gilt. £2 2s. net.

ORIENTAL LOWESTOFT

By J. A. Lloyd Hyde. Written with special reference to the trade with China and the porcelain decorated for the American market. Lavishly illustrated. £2 2s. net.

ENGLISH CONVERSATION PIECES

By Sacheverell Sitwell, author of "Southern Baroque," etc. A pictorial Survey of Domestic Portrait Groups and their Painters during the eighteenth and nineteenth centuries. With 6 Colour and 96 monochrome Plates illustrating the work of some 70 painters, famous and unknown, much of it before unpublished, and forming a vivid and attractive representation of contemporary social life and famous figures. With descriptive and historical notes. 4to, cloth, gilt. 21s. net.

NARRATIVE PICTURES

By Sacheverell Sitwell. This sister volume to the same author's popular "Conversation Pieces" makes a comprehensive study of the painting of anecdote and story in England during the last 200 years. The works of Hogarth, Gainsborough, Fuseli, Zoffany, Turner, Cotman, Rowlandson, Cruickshank, Tissot, Wilkie and Frith are illustrated in the 6 colour and over 120 monochrome illustrations. Crown 4to, cloth, gilt. 21s. net.

FRENCH PAINTING IN THE XIXth CENTURY

By James Laver. Containing 12 Plates in colour and 96 in monochrome, with Notes on painters and pictures by Michael Sevier, and a Postcript by Alfred Flechtheim. Both for its scholarship and illustration this book should form one of the finest and most definitive ever devoted to its great subject. The pictures illustrated are nearly all taken from private collections, either English, Continental or American. Crown 4to, Cloth, gilt. 21s. net.

CHINESE ART

Including an Introduction by ROGER FRY and articles on Painting, Sculpture, Bronzes, Ceramics, Textiles, Jade, Enamels and Lacquer, etc., by LAURENCE BINYON, OSVALD SIREN, BERNARD RACKHAM, A. F. KENDRICK and W. W. WINKWORTH. With 23 fine full-page coloured plates, beautifully reproduced, of outstanding examples in public and private collections, and including also between 70 and 80 Photographic Illustrations on 52 plates, and a number of line cuts in the text, with maps, marks, tables of dynasties, etc. Large royal 8vo, cloth. 15s. net.

THE BURLINGTON MAGAZINE MONOGRAPHS

NO. II.—SPANISH ART

An Introductory Review of Architecture, Painting, Sculpture, Textiles, Ceramics, Woodwork, Metalwork, by ROYALL TYLER, SIR CHARLES HOLMES and H. ISHERWOOD KAY, GEOFFREY WEBB, A. F. KENDRICK, B. RACKHAM and A. VAN DE PUT, BERNARD BEVAN, and P. DE ARTINANO, respectively. With a General Introduction by R. R. TATLOCK, late Editor of *The Burlington Magazine*. Illustrated by 120 large scale reproductions of Paintings, Decorative Art, Buildings, etc., including 9 Plates in full colour, comprising 280 pictures in all. Royal 4to, cloth. 25s. net.

NO. III.—GEORGIAN ART

A Survey of Art in England during the reign of George III, 1760-1820, by leading authorities. The Sections comprise: *Painting* by J. B. MANSON; *Architecture and Sculpture* by GEOFFREY WEBB; *Ceramics* by BERNARD RACKHAM; *Woodwork* by OLIVER BRACKETT; *Textiles* by A. F. KENDRICK; *Minor Arts* by LOUISE GORDON-STABLES. With an Introduction by ROGER FRY. The Illustrations include 6 Plates in colour and 64 in half-tone, comprising some 100 subjects. Royal 4to, cloth. 21st. net.

THE DRAWINGS OF ANTOINE WATTEAU, 1684-1721

By Dr. K. T. PARKER, of the Ashmolean Museum, Oxford, Editor of "Old Master Drawings." A full, original and critical Survey. Illustrated by 100 Collotype Reproductions of selected characteristic Drawings from private and public collections, many unpublished, a Frontispiece in colour and 16 of the master's most important pictures. 4to, cloth, gilt. £2 2s. net.

A HISTORY OF BRITISH WATER-COLOUR PAINTING

By H. M. CUNDALL, F.S.A. With a Foreword by Sir H. HUGHES-STANTON, P.R.W.S. A New and Cheaper Edition, revised and enlarged, of this important standard work, with 64 full-page Illustrations in colour, and a full biographical list, arranged alphabetically, of the principal English Water-colourists. Large Medium 8vo, cloth. 15s. net.

HISTORIC TEXTILE FABRICS

By RICHARD GLAZIER. Containing: Materials—The Loom—Pattern—Tapestries—Dyed and Printed Fabrics—Church Vestments, etc., with about 100 Plates from Photographs and from the Author's Drawings including 4 in colour, and 43 Line Diagrams, illustrating over 200 varieties of Textile Design. Large 8vo, cloth, gilt. 21s. net.

THE ART AND CRAFT OF OLD LACE

In all Countries, from the XVIth to the Early XIXth Centuries. By ALFRED VON HENNEBERG. With an Introduction by WILHELM PINDER. Containing a full original account of the Development of Style and an Analysis of Technique and Texture. Illustrated by 190 full-page plates, 8 in colour, giving 60 specimens from scale diagrams and 250 of the finest pieces of Old Lace. Large 4to, cloth, gilt. £3 3s. net.

FURNITURE FOR SMALL HOUSES

By PERCY A. WELLS. Containing 56 Plates of Designs reproduced from Photographs and Working Drawings by the Author, together with Illustrations in the text. Cheaper reissue. Small 4to, cloth, 7s. 6d. net.

THE ART AND CRAFT OF HOME MAKING

By EDWARD W. GREGORY. Containing Practical Hints and Information on such subjects as Taking a House—Wallpapers—Furnishing Various Rooms —Pictures—Kitchen—Heating—Carpets—Curtains—Things that Get Out of Order, etc. Containing 224 pages, with 9 Plates in full colour of decorative schemes, numerous Photographs of Interiors, and many Sketches, Plans and Diagrams. Second Edition revised. Square 8vo, cloth. 7s. 6d. net.

MODERN DECORATIVE ART

A Series of 200 examples of Interior Decoration, Furniture, Lighting, Fittings, and other Ornamental Features. By MAURICE S. R. ADAMS. The book is arranged in sections, taking in turn each type of room, and giving its complete furnishing. Illustrated by 120 photographic plates and line drawings, with descriptive text. Demy 4to, art canvas, gilt. 8s. 6d. net.

DESIGN IN WOODWORK

By PERCY A. WELLS, author of "Modern Cabinetwork," etc. Illustrated by 25 full-page drawings comprising 150 diagrams and 47 plates from photographs of Mirrors, Stools, Clocks, Cabinets, Tables, Bookcases, etc. Demy 8vo, cloth. 6s. net.

HANDCRAFT IN WOOD AND METAL

A Handbook for the use of Teachers, Students, Craftsmen, and others. By JOHN HOOPER and ALFRED J. SHIRLEY. With over 300 Illustrations from Drawings and Photographs. Fifth Edition, revised and enlarged. Large 8vo, cloth. 10s. 6d. net.

CRAFTWORK IN METAL

A Practical Elementary Textbook for Teachers, Students, and Workers. By ALFRED J. SHIRLEY. Comprising a series of progressive Lessons and Exercises, illustrated by numerous full-page Plates from the Author's Drawings, each accompanied by detailed working directions, including also Practical Notes, Tables, etc. Medium 8vo, cloth. 5s. net.

BOOKCRAFTS AND BOOKBINDING. A Practical Course.

By JOHN MASON, Teacher at Leicester College of Arts and Crafts, etc., Containing sections on Historical Developments, various Binding Processes, Lettering, Leather, Paper, etc., with some 300 illustrations from diagrams and photographs of operations and finished designs. Large 8vo, cloth. 8s. 6d. net.

WOODCRAFT: DESIGN AND PRACTICE

By RODNEY HOOPER. A practical manual which gives a variety of up-to-date and original treatments for the design and construction of domestic furniture and woodwork. There are 100 pages of text, more than 100 sketches and diagrams by the Author, comprising hundreds of practical drawings, and 40 photographs of furniture designed by the most eminent firms and individuals. Super royal 8vo, cloth. 12s. 6d. net.

PRACTICAL CRAFTWORK DESIGN

A SERIES OF PROGRESSIVE LESSONS AND EXAMPLES IN LEATHERWORK GLOVE-MAKING, RAFFIA, AND FELTWORK. By WINIFRED CLARKE, Teacher of Needlework and Leather at Loughborough College. With numerous plates in colour, half-tone and line from the author's designs, and from photographs of finished objects. Royal 8vo. Half-cloth. 7s. 6d. net.

COLOUR: A Manual of its Study and Practice

By H. Barrett Carpenter, late Headmaster of the School of Art, Rochdale. A Series of 16 concise but very practical chapters, based on the Author's experiments, on Harmony—Contrast—Discord—Keynotes—Intermingling—Effect of Lighting—Dirty Colour—Black-and-White, etc. Illustrated by 24 Plates (some double size), printed in colour; giving 40 Examples of Colour Combinations, Grading, Toning, etc., including some new examples in colour of application in Historic Design. New and Revised Impression. 8vo, cloth, gilt. 9s. net.

A COLOUR CHART

Issued in connection with the above book. Consisting of a circle 17 inches in diameter, printed in Graded Colour, showing 14 shades, Combinations and Contrasts. With explanatory letterpress. Folio, stout paper. 2s. 6d. net.

ALPHABETS, OLD AND NEW

With 224 complete Alphabets, 30 series of Numerals, many Ancient Dates, etc. Selected and Arranged by Lewis F. Day. With a short account of the Development of the Alphabet. Crown 8vo, cloth. 5s. net.

PEN PRACTICE

By Walter Higgins. Chapters on Tools, Broad-pen Practice, Spacing, Italics, Uncials and Half-uncials, Setting out, A Cursive Hand, etc. With 27 Plates specially drawn by the Author, giving some hundreds of Letters, Ornaments and Exercises, and 6 from selected Historical Examples. Second Edition, revised. Crown 8vo, paper covers, 1s. 6d. net; or boards 2s. 6d. net.

THE ROMAN ALPHABET AND ITS DERIVATIVES

A large-sized Reproduction of the Alphabet of the Trajan Column. By Allen W. Seaby. A Series of large Plates, printed from the wood blocks, and including typical examples of Renaissance, Gothic, and Modern Alphabets and Types. With Introduction and descriptive Notes. Medium 4to half-bound, or in portfolio. 4s. 6d. net.

101 THINGS FOR LITTLE FOLKS TO DO

By A. C. Horth, Editor of "Educational Handcraft," Examiner to the Board of Education, and author of numerous craftwork manuals. Containing sections on paper folding, cutting and making, and making many amusing and useful objects, painting, etc. With 90 full page practical diagrams by the author and a special series of 31 plates from designs in colour. An unfailing source of entertainment and instruction for young children of both sexes. Crown 8vo, cloth. 5s. net.

101 THINGS FOR GIRLS TO DO

By A. C. Horth, Editor of "Educational Handwork," etc. With practical sections on Stitchery, the making of decorative Household Articles in felt, leather, gesso, raffia, Hints on Mending, Cleaning, First-Aid, etc. Illustrated by numerous Line Diagrams, Photographs of finished objects, etc. Crown 8vo, cloth. 5s. net.

101 THINGS FOR A BOY TO MAKE

By A. C. Horth. With Notes on Workshop Practice and Processes, Tools, Joints, and full reliable directions for making Working Models. Illustrated by numerous full-page and smaller practical Diagrams and Sketches specially prepared. Second Edition, revised and enlarged. Crown 8vo cloth. 5s. net.

101 THINGS FOR THE HANDYMAN TO DO

By A. C. Horth. This highly useful volume has been designed for the use of the man who likes to do the odd jobs about the house. Like the other books in the series it is lavishly illustrated by hundreds of photographs, sketches and diagrams. Crown 8vo, cloth. 7s. 6d. net.

ART IN DAILY LIFE FOR YOUNG AND OLD

By D. D. SAWER, late Art Lecturer at the Diocesan College, Brighton. A companion and complement to the following work with a Foreword by P. H. JOWETT, A.R.C.A. A comprehensive course for Teachers, Students and Art Lovers; treating of the Place of Drawing, Plants and their Use, Figure Drawing and Drapery, Animal Drawing, Modelling Shapes and Figures, Casting, Clay Modelling, Object Drawing, Notes on Crafts, Composition, Design, applied and graphic. With 10 plates in colour and 200 illustrations in line and half-tone. Medium 8vo, cloth. 10s. 6d. net.

EVERYDAY ART AT SCHOOL AND HOME

By D. D. SAWER. With an appreciative Foreword by Sir Michael Sadler, C.B., Oxford. A Practical Course based on the new Board of Education "Suggestions to Teachers," and adaptable to Dalton Methods, containing graduated lessons on Design, Flower-painting, etc., with sections on Architectural Drawing, Lettering, Stained Glass, Leatherwork, and other Crafts. With 64 Plates in half-tone, from the Author's Drawings, numerous full-page and smaller Line Illustrations, and 8 Plates in colour. Second Edition, revised and enlarged. Medium 8vo, cloth. 10s. 6d. net.

PERSPECTIVE IN DRAWING

A simple Introductory Account. By D. D. SAWER. With an Introduction by Professor ALLEN W. SEABY, late Professor of Fine Art, University of Reading. With Sections on Basic Principles, the Cube, Cylinder, Shadows, Reflections, Aerial Perspective, Colour and Drawing. Illustrated by over 100 Diagrams and Sketches, a Frontispiece in colour, and reproductions from Photographs. Crown 8vo, cloth. 5s. net.

SKETCHING AND PAINTING FOR YOUNG AND OLD

An Elementary Practical Manual. By D. D. SAWER, with a Foreword by LORD BADEN-POWELL. With chapters on: Ungathered Wealth, a Day Out, Materials, Practice, the First Sketch Out of Doors, Composition, Mounting and Framing. Illustrated by a coloured Frontispiece, 8 plates in line and half-tone, and 31 text illustrations from the author's sketches, diagrams, etc. Crown 8vo, stiff covers, 1s. 6d. net; or quarter-cloth, 2s. net.

LAUGHS AND SMILES and How to Draw Them. By A. A. Braun, author of "Figures, Faces and Folds" and other works.

Containing 45 Plates, printed in tints, of numerous constructional sketches, building up in successive stages humorous likenesses of well-known personages. Comprising about 300 sketches, with concise text and anatomical diagrams. Oblong 4to, decorative boards, cloth back. 3s. 6d. net.

FIGURES, FACES AND FOLDS

For Fashion Artists, Dress Designers, and Art Students. By ADOLPHE ARMAND BRAUN. Containing 112 comparative Plates, giving over 300 Illustrations of Costume and Drapery. Including a special series of nude and draped studies from models specially posed for fashion work. With practical text, Dress diagrams, Figure details, Anatomy analysis, etc. Cheaper reissue. Demy 4to, stiff paper covers, 10s. 6d. net; cloth, gilt, 12s. 6d. net.

THE CHILD IN ART AND NATURE

By A. A. BRAUN. Containing chapters on Anatomy, Development, and Expression, and over 300 Illustrations from Photographs and Drawings of child poses, expressions, the Child Figure in Art. Second Edition. 4to, in stiff covers, 10s. 6d. net; or cloth, gilt, 12s. 6d. net.

A MANUAL OF HISTORIC ORNAMENT

Being an Account of the Development of Architecture and the Historic Arts, for the use of Students and Craftsmen. By RICHARD GLAZIER, A.R.I.B.A. Fifth Edition, revised and enlarged. Containing 700 Illustrations, chiefly from the Author's Pen Drawings, including many new to this Edition from various sources, and a special series of coloured and Photographic Plates of Ornament of the Orient and the Renaissance. Large 8vo. cloth. 12s. 6d. net.

A HANDBOOK OF ORNAMENT

By Professor F. SALES MEYER. With 3,000 Illustrations of the Elements and the Application of Decoration to Objects, e.g. Vases, Frets, Diapers, Consoles, Frames, Jewellery, Heraldry, etc., grouped on over 300 Plates, reproduced from the Author's specially prepared Drawings. With descriptive text to each subject. Large 8vo, cloth. 15s. net.

THE STYLES OF ORNAMENT

From Prehistoric Times to the Middle of the XIXth Century. A Series of 3,500 Examples Arranged in Historical Order, with descriptive text. By ALEXANDER SPELTZ. Revised and Edited by R. PHENÉ SPIERS, F.S.A., F.R.I.B.A. Containing 560 pages, with 400 full-page Plates exhibiting upwards of 3,500 separate Illustrations. Large 8vo, cloth, gilt. 15s. net.

ABSTRACT DESIGN

A Practical Manual on the Making of Pattern. By AMOR FENN, late Head of the Art Section, Goldsmith's College, New Cross. A series of careful, informative sections on Conditions, Elements, etc. Illustrated by about 180 full-page Designs from the Author's specially-prepared Drawings. 8vo, cloth, 12s. 6d. net.

PATTERN DESIGN

For Students, treating in a practical way the Anatomy, Planning, and Evolution of Repeated Ornament. By LEWIS F. DAY. Containing about 300 pages, and 300 practical Illustrations from specially prepared Drawings and Photographs of the Principles of Repeat Design, the "Drop," the "Spot" Geometrical Ornament, etc. New edition, revised and enlarged by AMOR FENN, with many fresh Illustrations, including a series in colour. Demy 8vo, cloth, gilt. 10s. 6d. net.

NATURE AND ORNAMENT

By LEWIS F. DAY. NATURE THE RAW MATERIAL OF DESIGN, treating chiefly of the decorative possibilities of Plant Form, its growth, features, and detail. With 350 Illustrations, chiefly grouped comparatively under Flowers, Seed Vessels, Fruits, Berries, etc., specially drawn by Miss J. FOORD. New and cheaper Edition, revised, with a Chapter by MARY HOGARTH. Demy 8vo, cloth. 5s. net.

DRAWING, DESIGN AND CRAFTWORK

For Teachers, Students, and Designers. By FREDK. J. GLASS. Containing 262 pages, with some 2,000 Illustrations on 156 Plates, from Drawings by the Author and others, and Historic Designs: Chinese, Persian, Japanese, Medieval, etc. Third Edition revised and enlarged with many new Plates, including a special series in colour of Historic and Modern Designs. Demy 8vo, cloth. 12s. net.

APPLIED ART

A Course of Study in Drawing, Painting, Design and Handicraft, arranged for the self-instruction of Teachers, Parents and Students. By P. J. LEMOS, Editor of *The School Arts Magazine*. Containing 400 pages lavishly illustrated by 37 Plates in colour and 246 in line, pencil, wash and half-tone, from specially-prepared drawings and photographs, comprising a total of over 3,000 illustrations. Large 8vo, cloth, gilt. 28s. net.

THE ART TEACHER

By P. J. LEMOS, Director of the Museum of Fine Arts, Leland Stanford Junior University, and Editor of *The School Arts Magazine*. A comprehensive compendium of Art Teaching Ideas, Suggestions and Methods based upon the practice of leading schools and colleges in the United States and other countries. Containing 500 pages, profusely illustrated by 68 Plates in colour and about 1,000 illustrations in line, pencil and wash from the author's specially-prepared drawings, together with photographs. Large 8vo, cloth. £2 net.

MUSIC THROUGH THE DANCE

By EVELYN PORTER, L.R.A.M., M.R.S.T. A handbook for teachers and students, showing how musical growth has been influenced by the dance throughout the ages. Illustrated by 22 half-tone plates and by numerous quotations in music. Dance Examples by MARJORIE WOOLNOTH and a Greek Dance by RUBY are also included. Medium 8vo, cloth. 7s. 6d. net.

MODELLING

By F. J. GLASS. Containing Chapters on Figure Modelling; Relief Work; Composition; Casting; Gelatine Moulding; etc. With a section on History and Ornament. Illustrated by about 30 Plates of stages and processes, 35 Plates of Sculpture and many Line Illustrations. Royal 8vo, cloth, gilt. 15s. net.

THE ART AND CRAFT OF LINO CUTTING AND PRINTING

By CLAUDE FLIGHT, author of "Tinker, Tailor," etc. With a Foreword by J. E. BARTON. Treating of Designing, Cutting, Printing, Alterations, etc. With 77 Illustrations, largely full-page, including 5 in full colour, by the author and others, and also diagrams and prints in various stages. Tall 8vo, decorative boards. 3s. 6d. net.

PRACTICAL WOODCARVING

By ELEANOR ROWE. Third Edition, revised and enlarged, in Two Parts; I. ELEMENTARY WOODCARVING, embodying "Hints on Woodcarving." With numerous Illustrations, many full-page, from Drawings and Photographs of carving operations, examples and details. II. ADVANCED WOODCARVING. With numerous Illustrations, many full-page from Drawings and Photographs of historic and modern carvings. Demy 8vo, limp cloth, lettered, 5s. net each; or two parts in one volume, cloth, gilt, 10s. net.

SAMPLERS AND STITCHES

A Handbook of the Embroiderer's Art. By MRS. ARCHIBALD CHRISTIE. Containing 40 full-page Reproductions from Photographs, a Frontispiece in colour, and 289 Text Drawings. Third Edition, revised and enlarged. Crown 4to, boards, canvas back. 25s. net.

MODERN DESIGN IN EMBROIDERY

By REBECCA CROMPTON, Examiner and Occasional Inspector in Women's Crafts to the Board of Education. Edited by DAVIDE C. MINTER. A novel approach to the craft on modern lines. With chapters on Creative Embroidery, the Value of Line, Fillings, Tone Value, Colour, etc. Illustrated by 4 Plates in colour, 74 Photographs of finished samplers, all specially designed and worked by the author, and 112 practical Line Diagrams in the text. Large 8vo, cloth, 8s. 6d. net.

STITCH PATTERNS AND DESIGNS FOR EMBROIDERY

By ANNE BRANDON-JONES. Containing 48 pages with 45 photographic examples on 12 Plates of simple and effective embroidery Motives, a Frontispiece in colour and numerous Text Illustrations of Stitches and Methods. Crown 4to, paper wrappers, 3s. net; or in cloth, 4s. net.

CANVAS EMBROIDERY

A Manual for Students and Amateurs by LOUISA F. PESEL. Containing 48 pages of text, a coloured Frontispiece, and 14 specially prepared Plates showing Stitches and methods. Medium oblong 4to, paper wrappers, 3s. net; or bound in cloth, 4s. net.

ENGLISH EMBROIDERY. I. DOUBLE-RUNNING, OR BACK-STITCH

By LOUISA F. PESEL. With coloured Frontispiece, 10 specially drawn Plates of 45 Working Designs, and 8 Plates from Photographs of 10 English and Coptic Samplers, comprising numerous Patterns and Motives. With Practical Text and a Preface by ETTA CAMPBELL, Embroidery Teacher, Winchester School of Arts. Uniform with "Canvas Embroidery." Large oblong 4to, paper wrappers, 3s. net; or boards, cloth back, 4s. net.

ENGLISH EMBROIDERY. II. CROSS-STITCH

By LOUISA F. PESEL. With a Coloured Frontispiece, 10 specially drawn Plates of 32 Working Designs, etc., and 8 Plates from Photographs of 15 typical English Samplers and Objects. Comprising 43 subjects, giving hundreds of Patterns and Motives. With Practical Text and a Preface by Professor R. GLEADOWE, late Slade Professor of Fine Arts, Oxford University. Large oblong 4to, paper wrappers, 3s. net; or boards, cloth back, 4s. net.

ILLUSTRATED STITCHERY DECORATIONS

By WINIFRED M. CLARKE. Containing 19 Plates from the Author's specially prepared Drawings, giving some 120 useful original Motives: Borders, Rosettes, Floral Elements, Patterns, Lettering and Worked Objects, such as Bags, Blotters, etc. Including a coloured Frontispiece, Introductory Text and full descriptive Notes on the Plates. Crown 4to, stiff paper wrappers, 3s. net; boards, cloth back, 4s. net.

ART IN NEEDLEWORK

A BOOK ABOUT EMBROIDERY. By LEWIS F. DAY and MARY BUCKLE. Fourth Edition, revised by MARY HOGARTH. Including a specially worked Series of Stitch-Samplers, numerous supplementary Diagrams and many Plates of Historic Embroidery—Chinese, Medieval, Italian, French and Modern English. With additional Examples of Modern Work by DUNCAN GRANT, MRS. NEWALL, MRS. STOLL, D. HAGER, and others. Containing 280 pages, 80 full-page Plates, reproduced from Photographs, and 50 Illustrations in the text. Crown 8vo, cloth. 7s. 6d. net.

THE "PRACTICAL DRAWING" SERIES

COMPOSITION

An Analysis of the Principles of Pictorial Design. By CYRIL C. PEARCE, R.B.A. With chapters on Tone, Distribution, Gradation, Scale, Perspective, Rhythm, Harmony and Balance of Colour, Discords. Illustrated by 130 sketches and diagrams, 6 plates in colour, and 28 full-page illustrations from great masters. Med. 8vo. 10s. 6d. net.

ANIMAL ANATOMY AND DRAWING

By EDWIN NOBLE. Illustrated by a series of Plates in facsimile of the Author's Drawings of HORSES, CATTLE, DOGS, BIRDS and WILD ANIMALS, representing also Features, Details, etc. Including also numerous full-page and smaller line drawings of Muscles, Bones, etc. Med. 8vo. 10s. 6d. net.

PEN DRAWING

A Practical Manual on Materials, Technique, Style, Texture, etc. By G. M. ELLWOOD. Containing sections on History—Technique—Materials—Figures, Faces and Hands—Style and Methods—Landscape and Architecture—Modern Work—Magazine Illustration—Humorous Drawing Advertisements—Fashion. With 100 pages of illustrations by the chief pen draughtsmen of present and recent times. Med. 8vo. 10s. 6d. net.

THE ART AND PRACTICE OF SKETCHING

A Comprehensive Treatise on the Practice of Sketching by every method. By JASPER SALWEY, A.R.I.B.A. The Author deals successively with various media—Pen, Pencil, Water-colour, Oil, Wash, Crayon, Chalk, etc., and gives a complete account of the Technique of each. Illustrated by 64 plates of half-tone illustration and 6 plates in colour, from the work of great artists. Med. 8vo. 10s. 6d. net.

THE ART OF DRAWING IN LEAD PENCIL

By JASPER SALWEY, A.R.I.B.A. A Practical Manual dealing with Materials, Technique, Notes and Sketching, Building up, Form and Style, Process Reproduction, etc. Second Edition, revised and enlarged. Containing 232 pages with 122 reproductions of selected pencil drawings of Land and Seascapes, Figure-Studies, Book-Illustrations, etc. Med. 8vo. 10s. 6d. net.

SKETCHING IN LEAD PENCIL

By JASPER SALWEY, A.R.I.B.A. An Introduction to the same author's "Art of Drawing in Lead Pencil," but dealing entirely with sketching as differentiated from the making of finished Drawings. A practical manual for the Architect, Student and Artist. Containing 111 pages and 56 Illustrations, by well-known artists in the medium, and by the author. 7s. 6d. net.

SKETCHING FROM NATURE

A Practical Treatise on the Principles of Pictorial Composition. By F. J. GLASS. CONTENTS: Choice of Subject and Planning of Sketch—Tones—Exercise in Composition—Examples from the Old Masters. With 6 Plates in colour, numerous compositions from the Author's Drawings, and a series by past masters of Landscape Painting. Med. 8vo. 10s. 6d. net.

DRAWING FOR ART STUDENTS AND ILLUSTRATORS

By ALLEN W. SEABY. Containing 220 pages, with 133 Illustrations printed in Sepia, mostly full-page Plates, from Drawings by Old and Modern Artists. Second Edition, revised and enlarged. 8vo, cloth. 10s. 6d. net.

ART AND UNDERSTANDING

By MARGARET H. BULLEY (M. H. Armitage), Lecturer and Examiner on Art, author of "Art and Counterfeit," etc. A comparative survey of the ideas underlying art, old and modern, pictorial and decorative, true and false, contrasting achievements and failures, &c. With 20 chapters on (*inter alia*) Psychology, Technique, Function, Form, etc.; full comments on the Illustrations; and a miniature anthology of striking quotations, prose and verse. Including 275 Illustrations of paintings, drawings, architecture, decorative objects, etc., from the work of primitive races, children, and masters old and new. Large 8vo, cloth. 15s. net.

FASHION DRAWING AND DESIGN

By LOUIE E. CHADWICK. Illustrated by numerous examples of Historic Fashion Plates, Explanatory Sketches by the Author, Figure Studies, and a series of about 80 full-page and double Plates of Contemporary Fashion Drawings by well-known artists. Large 8vo, cloth. 7s. 6d. net.

LIVING SCULPTURE

A Record of Expression in the Human Figure. By BERTRAM PARK and YVONNE GREGORY. With an historical and descriptive Introduction by G. MONTAGUE ELLWOOD. Comprising a Series of 47 full-page Studies of Selected Male and Female Figures with descriptive Notes. Small 4to, cloth, gilt. 12s. 6d. net.

ROUND THE WORLD IN FOLK TALES

A Regional Treatment. By RACHEL M. FLEMING. 16 Tales from Iceland, Mexico, Africa, Australia, etc., told in a fresh, easy style. With 17 illustrations from drawings and photographs. 8vo, boards 2s. net; cloth, 3s. net.

DINNER BUILDING

A Book of entertaining and practical instruction in the Noble Arts of Cooking and Eating. Written by W. TEIGNMOUTH SHORE. With an Introduction by GILBERT FRANKAU. A series of 42 bright, stimulating but practical Talks on such subjects as The Perfect Dinner, Sandwichery, Remnant Days, Cabbages and Things, incorporating hundreds of fresh recipes of all kinds. Cheaper reissue. F'cap 8vo, cloth, lettered. 2s. net.

THE "SHELL" GUIDES TO THE COUNTIES OF ENGLAND

Each containing from 50 to 60 pages, illustrated mainly by photographs, with map. 4to, in flexible binding. 2s. 6d. net each.

Volumes ready include:
CORNWALL; DERBYSHIRE; DEVON; DORSET; KENT; SOMERSET; WILTSHIRE; BUCKINGHAMSHIRE; HAMPSHIRE; NORTHUMBERLAND and DURHAM (in one volume).

BATSFORD'S PICTORIAL GUIDES TO EUROPEAN CITIES

I. STOCKHOLM. II. COPENHAGEN. III. AMSTERDAM. IV. HAMBURG.

Their Layout, Highways, Byways and Waterways, Distinctive Buildings, Life, Work and Play, presented in a series of some 100 attractive modern photographs, specially taken by Geoffrey Gilbert. With Tourist information and full informative captions. Square 8vo, in stiff covers. 2s. 6d. net per volume.

BATSFORD'S COLLECTORS' LIBRARY

A Series of Handbooks written by experts, providing information practical value to Connoisseurs, Collectors, Designers, and Students. Each volume forms an ideal introduction to its subject, and is fully illustrated by Reproductions in Colour and from Photographs. The following volumes are still available. 8vo, cloth, gilt, price 6s. net each.

OLD ENGLISH FURNITURE. By F. FENN and B. WYLLIE. With 94 Illustrations. *New Impression.*

OLD PEWTER. By MALCOLM BELL. With 106 Illustrations.

SHEFFIELD PLATE. By BERTIE WYLLIE. With 121 Illustrations.

FRENCH FURNITURE. By ANDRÉ SAGLIO. With 59 Illustrations.

DUTCH POTTERY AND PORCELAIN. By W. P. KNOWLES. With 54 Illustrations.

PORCELAIN. By WILLIAM BURTON. With 50 full-page Plates illustrating 87 examples from various Countries and Periods.

ENGLISH QUILTING, OLD AND NEW

A CONCISE REVIEW by ELIZABETH HAKE. With an Historical Account and Practical Directions for working. Illustrated from numerous Diagrams of Patterns and Tools, and some 50 photographs of selected examples from Devon and Somerset, Wales, Durham, and abroad, and of present-day working. 4to boards, 5s. 6d. net; cloth, 6s. 6d. net.

THE NEW INTERIOR DECORATION

By DOROTHY TODD and RAYMOND MORTIMER. With over 200 Illustrations on 96 Plates of Interiors of every sort, Furniture, Carpets, Textiles, Lighting, Wall Painting, etc., of the new school by such Architects and Artists as Le Corbusier, Mallet-Stevens, Gropius, Oud, Duncan Grant, Lescaze, etc. With descriptive text. Demy 4to, art canvas. 12s. 6d. net.

THE R.M.S. QUEEN MARY

A Picture Record of the great Steamship, 1930-1936. From Photographs by STEWART BALE and others. With Introduction and descriptive notes by GEORGE BLAKE, author of "The Shipbuilders," etc. With fine views of construction, trials, machinery, saloons, cabins, fittings, etc. Square 8vo, 4to cloth, pictorial sides, 2s. 6d. net; or full leather gilt, 5s. net.

THE BOOK OF SPEED

With 165 superb Illustrations in photogravure. Including: The Quest of Speed by STEPHEN KING-HALL; The Dawn of Flight by Col. ETHERTON; Speed in the Air by G. DE HAVILAND; "400 Miles an Hour!" by Flight-Lt. G. H. STAINFORTH; Motor Record Breaking by G. E. T. EYSTON; "What It Feels Like!" by Sir MALCOM CAMPBELL; Speed-Boats by H. SCOTT-PAINE; Motor-Cycle Racing by JAMES GUTHRIE; Speed by Rail by CECIL J. ALLEN The Ocean Routes by Sir A. ROSTRON; Speed in Warfare by Maj.-Gen. FULLER. 4to, cloth. 5s. net.

SPEED ON SALT

By GEORGE EYSTON and W. F. BRADLEY. With a Foreword by SIR MALCOLM CAMPBELL. A graphic first-hand review of their pioneer record-breaking motor-runs on the Bonneville Salt Flats, Utah, U.S.A., including the world's land speed record of 300 m.p.h., and the world's 24-hour record. With 132 attractive illustrations from special photographs of machines and men. Frontispiece in colour and coloured jacket by BRIAN COOK. 4to, cloth. 5s. net.

INDEX TO AUTHORS' NAMES AND SERIES

Printed in Great Britain by The Stanhope Press Ltd., Rochester, Kent.

```
            103570
DA      Brown, Ivor.
630         The heart of
.B77    England.
1935
```

DATE DUE